THE NEW GEOPOLITICS
of
EURASIA
and
TURKEY'S POSITION

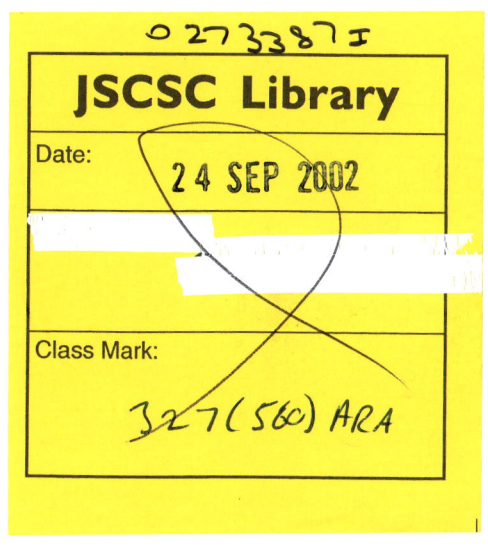

To my parents,
Gaffer Aras
and
Sevgili Aras

THE NEW GEOPOLITICS
of
EURASIA
and
TURKEY'S POSITION

BÜLENT ARAS

With a Foreword by Barry Rubin

FRANK CASS
LONDON   PORTLAND, OR

First published in 2002 in Great Britain by
FRANK CASS PUBLISHERS
Crown House, 47 Chase Side, Southgate, London N14 5BP

and in the United States of America by
FRANK CASS PUBLISHERS
c/o ISBS, 5824 N.E. Hassalo Street
Portland, Oregon 97213-3644

Website: www.frankcass.com

British Library Cataloguing in Publication Data

Aras, Bülent
The new geopolitics of Eurasia and Turkey's position
1. Geopolitics – Eurasia 2. Geopolitics – Turkey 3. Eurasia –
Foreign relations 4. Turkey – Foreign relations – 1980 –
I. Title
327.1'095

ISBN 0-7146-5075-7 (cloth)
ISBN 0-7146-8122-9 (paper)

Library of Congress Cataloging-in-Publication Data

Aras Bülent
The new geopolitics of Eurasia and Turkey's position / Bülent Aras;
with a foreword by Barry Rubin.
      p. cm.
Includes bibliographical references and index.
ISBN 0-7146-5075-7 (cloth) – ISBN 0-7146-8122-9 (pbk.)
      1. Caspian Sea Region – Foreign relations – Turkey. 2. Turkey – Foreign
relations – Caspian Sea Region. 3. Asia, Central – Foreign relations – Turkey.
4. Turkey – Foreign relations – Asia, Central. 5. Geopolitics – Caspian Sea
Region. 6. Geopolitics – Asia, Central. I. Title.

DK509 .A69 2002
327.5610475'0949 – dc21

                                                                                    2002071595

Typeset in in 10.25/12pt Times New Roman
Printed in Great Britain by MPG Books Ltd
Victoria Square, Bodmin, Cornwall

CONTENTS

LIST OF TABLES

FOREWORD

A new region has entered onto the international scene. This area does have a historical identity and a set of issues that bind it together. Yet what should this area be called and how does it relate to neighboring regions? The difficulty in answering these two questions indicates the volatility of a land mass still in search of a role and cohesion.

For example, one might label this place the 'former southern republics of the Soviet Union', but this refers to a situation that no longer exists and might be viewed as a 75-year detour from their normal existence and long-term destiny. The term Eurasian, too, stresses that this region can go in more than one direction. In an equal sense, it is the northern edge of the Middle East, too. Or one can divide this area into two by calling it the Caucasus and Central Asia. Yet the latter designation equally begs the question. What, after all, does 'Central Asia' mean? Certainly, those particular states and societies do not relate mainly to China, Japan or India.

Moreover, this cannot be called a Muslim region since that excludes Armenia and Georgia, nor a Turkic one, since that excludes those two specific countries plus Tajikistan as well. Indeed, despite aspects of Muslim and Turkic identity, these countries are trying to build nation-states based on an ethnic character that in most cases goes back for many centuries.

Of course, these semantic issues indicate some of the area's key features. It stands between more than one region and continent, a choice involving both options and temptations. Further, the coming together of so many ethnic and religious mixtues – remembering also that each of these countries also has large minority groups – is the source of real or potential political problems. In addition, while ethnic groups are old, the states are new. National identities must be constructed or rebuilt in an effort to find a way to establish stable countries.

As if these internal pressures were not enough, the area has become an important front for competition by several great powers, inspired by both strategic rivalry and a desire to participate in exploiting the region's new-found oil and gas reserves.

On one hand, there is the purely economic level, in which Turkey, Russia and Iran vie for petroleum supplies and profits. This involves questions over the ownership of oil and gas fields – which is tied up with mineral rights in the Caspian Sea, too – and pipeline routes. Some observers, however, question the whole basis of this argument, noting that reserves may be overestimated while production and transport arrangements will be difficult and costly.

On the other hand, these same three states are to a certain extent competing – though cooperation is also possible – for some sphere of influence over this region. Outside powers, most obviously the United States, have joined in. In the American case, the opposition to any strengthening of Iran has also become a factor.

Turkey has on its side an ethnic appeal to many of these states, as well as furnishing them with a model for development. Russia, the former ruler, has greatly influenced the current nature of these places and may appeal – as savior or bully – as a factor for the survival or accession of particular regimes. Iran has the Islam card, and is also able to sponsor political and social movements.

In particular, Turkey perceived the Soviet Union's dissolution and sudden appearance of these new states as a source of potential opportunity as well as risk. Ankara presented itself as a secular role model for the republics in their struggle too jettison the Soviet legacy and fully integrate themselves into the world order. As a result, Turkey sought to develop a sphere of influence abroad for the first time in its republican history.

The timing of these events was fortuitious in both strategic and economic terms. Turkey needed to rethink its foreign policy after the Cold War to avoid losing its strategic importance to the West, especially the United States. Turkey also hoped to find guaranteed access to vital energy resources, lucrative oil and gas transport revenues and new markets for Turkish goods, especially in Azerbaijan, Turkmenistan and Kazakhstan. It has been estimated that Turkey will have to import roughly 55 million tons of oil annually by the year 2010 to maintain the present course of its economic development.

What exists, then, is a range of domestic and international factors that make instability possible, but by no means inevitable, in this area.

Bülent Aras's work is an excellent guide through this area's intricacies and still-coalescing forces. He examines these countries as entities in their own right and not just as future popeline routes or oilfields with borders. Dr Aras has a long and detailed familiarity with these countries, which he has frequently visited and several of whose languages he speaks.

There are not many parts of the world whose destiny is as open and fate so undetermined as this one. Given this fact, and the growing importance of the region, Bülent Aras's book is especially welcome and useful.

Barry Rubin

INTRODUCTION

This book is an attempt to analyze new geopolitics of the Eurasia within the context of the global and regional involvement to this region. Turkey's position vis-à-vis new geopolitics of Eurasia may provide insights for the future route of Turkish foreign policy toward the region. In addition, the analysis of the foreign involvement to the region may also help to understand likely developments in the land mass of the newly emerging Eurasian countries.

A series of geopolitical relationships are emerging in Eurasia. On one side are Russia and Iran along with a series of smaller powers, including Greece and Armenia. On the other side are Turkey, Azerbaijan, Georgia, Ukraine and, as recent developments indicate, Israel. Also on the rise in the region is the influence and engagement of the United States and the European Union, both of which seek to tap into the vast energy reserves of the Caspian region. The emerging security environment is thus one in which two blocs of states are in increasing competition with each other. Therefore, policies that promote the further emergence of a bipolar order will have the potential to aggravate regional tensions and introduce new security concerns in this important yet unstable region.

Turkey has been among the few states that have shown a great interest in the Turkic republics of the former Soviet Union after their emergence onto the stage of world politics. The dissolution of the Soviet state and the sudden appearance of these new states on the former Soviet periphery were all perceived by Turkey as a source of potential opportunity as well as risk.[1] Throughout the course of time, it became apparent that this interest is not one-sided but involves a complex pattern of relations, rather than simply representing Ankara's attempt to spread Turkish influence and guarantee Turkish security.

After the dissolution of the Soviet state, for the first time in its republican history, Turkey sought to develop a sphere of influence. It moved to capitalize on the common historical and linguistic ties that it has with the republics of the former Soviet Union, the only exception being Tajikistan, whose population is predominantly Farsi-speaking. The historical links between the Turks and the peoples of Central Asia and Azerbaijan developed over centuries through migration and intermingling and now provide the basis for a mutual attraction and, therefore, the development of relations between Turkey and the Muslim former Soviet republics.[2] In addition to common historical and linguistic ties, Ankara has also presented itself as a model to these countries that they could adopt in their struggle to get rid of the Soviet legacy and integrate themselves into the modern world system.[3] In other words, Ankara sought to fill a gap that arose following upon the break-up of the Soviet Union, and has portrayed itself as a potential big brother to the newly independent republics.

At the time of the collapse of the Soviet Union, there was a widespread belief that Turkey was losing its strategic importance in the eyes of Western policy makers, especially the US. Turkey's government decided to ally itself with the NATO powers following upon the close of World War Two and the birth of the Cold War and, although it has experienced difficult periods in its relations with the West, it nonetheless maintained an undeniable strategic importance as an ally against Communism. Primary among the concerns of Turkish policy-makers was that, with the end of the Cold War, Turkey would become increasingly irrelevant to the West, thereby losing out on its long-standing dream of full integration with a united Europe.[4] Finding a new role for Turkey within the overall framework of Western strategy that would guarantee Turkey's continued importance became a central preoccupation of Ankara.[5] Turkish policy-makers began to market the idea that Turkey could serve as a secular model to the newly independent Turkic republics, thereby profiting from the undeniable cultural, linguistic, and religious affinities between the Turkish people and the people of these new nations.[6] This view presented Turkic-speaking people as, in a sense, a single people, ranging from Asia Minor to Asia proper.

Another important asset in Turkey's quest for a new identity in the context of a new Eurasian geopolitical scenario is its economic potential. Turkey had profited from its alliance with the West during the Cold War. Now, with that conflict at an end, it has been seeking to capitalize on the establishment of ties with the countries of the former Soviet Union. These opportunities include guaranteed access to vital energy resources, lucrative oil transport revenues and new potential markets for Turkish goods, as well as increased diplomatic clout and strategic importance. For the new Turkic-speaking republics, Turkey offers them the prospect of attracting investment and technological expertise, as well as establishing a secure route for the distribution of their products to the West. Among the newly independent states, Azerbaijan, Turkmenistan and Kazakhstan – the Turkic-speaking former Soviet states of the Caspian region – have attracted the greatest interest on the part of Turkey.[7] The reason for of

2

this interest is not only the linguistic, ethnic, religious and cultural affinities shared by Turkey with these countries, but also the tremendous oil and gas reserves possessed by the Caspian states. It is not difficult to understand why Turkey has oil on its mind. It has been estimated that, to maintain the present course of its economic development, Turkey will require the importation of vast amounts of crude oil in coming decades – roughly 22 million tons annually by the year 2010.[8]

The key to Turkey's ambitions with respect to the newly independent states was recognized to be the Transcaucasus – in particular Azerbaijan. As a crossroads among land masses, Transcaucasia offers Turkey access to the republics of Central Asia. Serving as a bridgehead to the east is Azerbaijan, important to Turkey in its own right due to its large oil reserves and its 7.5 million population of Azerbaijani Turks, the closest relatives to the Anatolian Turks of all the Turkic peoples of the former Soviet Union.[9]

With the dissolution of the Soviet Union, academics and political analysts put forward the idea that a geopolitical vacuum had emerged in this region and that Turkey, Iran and Russia would be among the major competitors seeking to fill this vacuum. This idea of 'filling the vacuum' in the Caucasus and Central Asia was not generated in Ankara's think tanks. It was the result of a handful of articles and papers penned by well-known American specialists (such as those at the Rand Corp. and the Heritage Foundation), which were quickly picked up and repeated by influential press organs (*New York Times, Washington Post*, etc.). This new strategy – which had a multitude of objectives, such as rewarding Turkey, acknowledging the role of language and history and thwarting a mythical Islamic threat to the region – was being embraced in Europe, the United States and, of course, Turkey itself. Official Ankara grabbed onto it and ran as fast and as far as it could, hoping and expecting that the rhetoric was going to turn into cold cash, not to mention long-term influence.

The Western media often published articles on various alliances that might be able to prevent the extension of Iranian influence into Azerbaijan and the new republics of Central Asia. Those articles argued that several pro-Western Islamic countries – notably Turkey, Pakistan, Egypt and Saudi Arabia – appeared to have undertaken significant efforts to establish ties with the newly independent Islamic countries to counter Iranian influence.[10] In this sense, Turkey's moves into Central Asia and Azerbaijan were aimed against the spread of 'fundamentalist' Islamic ideas there. Turkey's willingness to accept this role to promote a secular-democratic model in this area was a matter of "cultural correctness' as well as political strategy. The articles and policy statements emphasizing Turkey's 'Western identity' were encouraging and a sort of endorsement in terms of the success of Westernization in the eyes of foreign-policymakers. This new policy line was also in conformity with the ideology of the Turkish establishment due to its understanding of Islam as a

3

significant other in the domestic political domain. Interestingly, the main success of Turkey so far in this newly emerging area is the presence and activities of its civil society, non-governmental organizations and business interests, other than attempts of official Ankara.

This notion of Turkey's central mission as crucial to the future of Central Asia has been based, however, on an exaggerated view of Turkey's capabilities as well as an acute lack of understanding concerning the nature of these newly emerging 'kindred' countries, their expectations and objectives. Similarly, there is very little that Iranians are doing or are able to do with respect to spreading their message of Islam outside of Tajikistan. All of these states (with the exception of Tajikistan, which is still in a state of civil war among Islamic groups) in Central Asia are carrying out anti-Islamist policies. Thus, if there is any competition between Iran and Turkey, it is in the areas of trade and commerce and not in exporting (or preventing the dissemination of) Islam to Central Asia. Ignoring their weaknesses and overestimating their strengths, Tehran and Ankara committed major mistakes in the former Soviet south. As Igor P. Lipovsky pointed out, 'neither Turkey nor Iran were able to take on Russia's previous role in the region'.[11] The new states of Central Asia and Azerbaijan turned their faces toward Europe and the United States and to some extent to the Far Eastern countries. Therefore, even if there is a desire for competition between Turks and Iranians, they may not have the willing audience that they need.

Turkey has been a close ally of the United States for the last four decades. Iran is more than uncomfortable with having a neighbor allied with its main enemy. Given Turkey's pro-Western and secular orientation, Iran perceives Turkey as a 'Westoxicated' regime, subservient to the interests of the United States in the region. Turkey received an early endorsement from the US administration in the 'Turkish–Iranian competition' and an acknowledgment as the foremost vanguard against the spread of 'Islamic fundamentalism' among the newly independent Caucasian and Central Asian countries.

State identity in the context of world politics is mostly a product of domestic political contentions and social practices that both enable and restrain a state's interest and actions in foreign policy. Intersubjective relations – interactions and dialogue – in international politics are important in terms of identity formulations with both their material and discursive stamps. In this case, Turkish foreign-policymakers have paid special attention to the roles attributed to them and have shown a willingness to reshape this Western-constructed image in the process of reproducing identity through social practices and political-ideological contests at home. This will to manifest a national identity underscores the importance of others for the process of developing a self-understanding, although it seems more and more ironic in light of pending relations with the European Union.

Following this introduction, the first chapter is dedicated to an analysis of

Turkey's policy toward the Caspian Sea basin. After a brief section on Caspian controversies, Iranian and Russian policies are touched upon from a historical perspective. Following this discussion, I move into recent discussions on the nature of Turkish–American alliance in this region.

In the second and third chapters, I analyze Greece's security dilemma in the Caucasus and Iranian policy toward the Caspian Sea region basin. These chapters deal with the roles of both domestic and state-level actors in determining and pursuing relations. It pays special attention to regional and international contexts, mainly focusing on the roles of other nations in facilitating and obscuring political relations. Each chapter has a background section on the development of bilateral relations, and then moves into diverse, sophisticated political relations. In addition to attempting to construct an analytical explanation, these chapters also focus on Turkey's position.

The fourth chapter examines Israeli strategy in Azerbaijan and Central Asia. First, I give an overview of the new overall Israeli foreign-policy strategy as it has taken shape in the 1990s. Then, I demonstrate why the new republics of Central Asia have drawn the interest of Israel and have assumed an important priority in Israel's overall foreign policy. I also discuss why the prospect of expanded and improved relations with Israel has appeal for these new republics.

In the fifth and sixth chapters, I discuss the potential for further political and economic relations and cooperation, respectively, between the US and Central Asia, and European Countries and Turkic republics. I also analyze the prospects for Turkey to facilitate relations, focusing on policy preferences and alternatives in regional and international contexts. Both chapters end with a general overview of further potential cooperation, in the realms of both politics and economics.

The final chapter is dedicated to a general overview of the book and Turkey's policy options from a broad geopolitical perspective. I hold the idea that Turkey's new policy should be formulated in such a way as to take into account the Eurasian region as an international region, paying attention to the geopolitical realities of this vast area. For this purpose, I propose some alternative policies inspired by this approach with the goal in mind of overcoming some of the current problems associated with Turkey's policy toward the Caucasus and Central Asia.

NOTES

1. Stephen J. Blank, 'Turkey's Strategic Engagement in the Former USSR and US Interests', in Stephen J. Blank, Stephen C. Pelletiere and William T. Johnsen (eds), *Turkey's Strategic Position at the Crossroads of World Affairs* (Carlisle Barracks, PA: Strategic Studies Institute, 3 December 1993), p.55.
2. Graham E. Fuller, 'Turkey's New Eastern Orientation', in Graham E. Fuller and Ian O. Lesser (eds), *Turkey's New Geopolitics: From the Balkans to Western China* (Boulder: Westview Press, 1993), pp.67, 84.

3. Andrew Apostolou, 'New Players in an Old Game', *The Middle East*, No. 213 (July 1992), p.5.
4. Michael P. Croissant, 'Turkey and NATO After the Cold War', *Strategic Review* 23, No. 4 (Fall 1995), p.67.
5. Shireen Hunter, *The Transcaucasus in Transition: Nation-Building and Conflict* (Washington, DC: Center for Strategic and International Studies, 1994), p.162.
6. Ian O. Lesser, 'Bridge or Barrier? Turkey and the West After the Cold War', in Fuller and Lesser (eds), *Turkey's New Geopolitics*, p.128.
7. Gareth M. Winrow, 'Turkey's Role in Asian Pipeline Politics', *Jane's Intelligence Review* 9, No. 2, (February 1997).
8. Temel Iskit, 'Turkey: A New Actor in the Field of Energy Politics', *Perceptions* 1, No. 1 (March–May 1996), p.66.
9. Kenneth Mackenzie, 'Azerbaijan and the Neighbors', *World Today* 48, No. 1 (January 1992), p.2; and Philip Robins, 'Between Sentiment and Self-Interest: Turkey's Policy Toward Azerbaijan and the Central Asian States', *Middle East Journal* 47, No. 4 (Autumn 1993), p.597.
10. Ironically, when Turkey was surfacing as a model to the Turkic republics, the most secular and Westernized (blue-eyed and blond-haired) Islamic population of Europe was facing onslaught due to their Ottoman–Islamic heritage by anti-Western and anti-secularist Serbs. For more information, see Mujeeb Khan, 'External Threats and the Promotion of a Trans-National Islamic Consciousness: The Case of the Late Ottoman Empire and Contemporary Turkey', *Islamic World Report* 1, No.1 (1996).
11. Igor P. Lipovsky, 'Central Asia: In Search of a New Political Identity', *Middle East Journal* 50, No. 2 (Spring 1996), p.223.

1

TURKEY'S POLICY TOWARD THE CASPIAN SEA REGION BASIN

The appearance of new states in Central Asia and the Caucasus region at the collapse of the Soviet Union caused a radical shift in the foreign policy of Turkey, and triggered a search for means of tactical political-economic penetration into these countries.[1] Turkey's efforts in this regard have been motivated by a desire to spread the Turkish model of government and society – consisting of parliamentary democracy, relatively free-market economy, and secularism in a Muslim society – as well as to take advantage of the mutual development opportunities that cooperation can create. For Turkey these opportunities include guaranteed access to vital energy resources and lucrative oil transport revenues, as well as increased diplomatic clout and strategic importance. For the new republics these opportunities include the prospect of attracting investment and technological expertise, as well as of establishing a secure route for distribution of their products to the West.

Azerbaijan, Turkmenistan, and Kazakhstan – the Turkic-speaking former Soviet states of the Caspian region – have attracted the greatest interest on the part of Turkey among the newly independent states. The source of this interest is not only the linguistic, ethnic, religious and cultural affinity shared by Turkey and these countries, but also the tremendous oil and gas reserves possessed by the Caspian states.

It is not difficult to understand why Turkey has oil on its mind. It has been estimated that, to maintain the present course of its economic development, Turkey will require the importation of vast amounts of crude oil in the coming decades – roughly 55 million tons annually by the year 2010.[2] But as the Turkish president said recently: 'We see this rich region of oil and gas reserves not just as a source of energy, but as an element of stability. Just as the founders of the European community saw coal as a source of peace and stability for Europe, so we see oil and gas in our region serving the same role.'[3] Turkey knows that forging trade and investment links with Azerbaijan and throughout the region will facilitate good relations and create an atmosphere of cooperation, which may go a long way toward preventing petty squabbling and opportunistic land-grabs among the ethnically and religiously diverse states that occupy the Caucasus and Central Asia.

Yet since these states gained their independence in the early 1990s and the first talk of developing their phenomenal oil reserves began, multiple controversies have arisen that have delayed implementation of various strategies for exploitation, and that have at least temporarily frustrated both Turkish and Azerbaijani ambitions. These controversies are by no means limited in their implications to Turkey and Azerbaijan, or even to the region as a whole. Rather, they have caught up dozens of players – both at the national level and below – which stand to benefit, or lose, from the successful exploitation of Caspian deposits. This study addresses these controversies, discusses the players involved in them, and offers some limited suggestions for their resolution.

CASPIAN CONTROVERSIES

The Azerbaijani Oil Controversies

The countries involved in the legal-status dispute of the exploitation of the Caspain Sea resources are all convinced that the anticipated revenue from the exploitation of the Caspian's mineral reserves will provide a significant boost to their economies and bring in much-needed foreign currency. But, owing to its small size and relatively low level of economic development, perhaps the country that stands to gain or lose the most is Azerbaijan.

The Azerbaijani government has asserted that development of Caspian shelf deposits will turn around its lagging economy and allow it to alleviate the suffering caused by the ongoing conflict that began in the early 1990s with neighboring Armenia over the disputed Nagorno-Karabakh region. Doubtless, Azerbaijan also hopes that the ownership of massive energy deposits will bring it into a position of greater strategic significance, thereby boosting its currently weak diplomatic bargaining power vis-à-vis energy-hungry states around the globe, including the United States and members of the European Union. The ideal outcome from the perspective of Azerbaijan would surely be to induce these countries to pressure Armenia into settling the Nagorno-Karabakh dispute in a manner favorable to Azerbaijan, ending the Armenian occupation of some 20 per cent of its territory.[4]

The people of Azerbaijan simultaneously suffer from despair over the Armenian occupation of Nagorno-Karabakh and feel burgeoning confidence in the country's future as a major oil producer.[5] The Azerbaijani government has vigorously set about trying to realize the country's oil ambitions. Its first move was to begin negotiations through the State Oil Company of the Azerbaijan Republic (SOCAR) with a group of foreign oil companies in the first years of independence, culminating in the signing of a deal on 4 June 1994 that has been widely dubbed the 'Contract of the Century', worth around $8 billion.[6]

Officially named the 'Agreement on the Joint Development and Production Sharing for the Azeri and Chirag Fields and the Deep Water Portion of the Gunashli Field in the Azerbaijan Sector of the Caspian Sea', the contract called for the establishment of a business entity known as the Azerbaijan International Operating Company (AIOC), whose purpose is to exploit some of the richest oil reserves over which Azerbaijan claims sovereignty. The shares of the AIOC consortium are currently divided between SOCAR and foreign companies. Originally, SOCAR was to have a 20 per cent share, which would have given it a majority interest, but it subsequently transferred 5 per cent of the total shares to Turkish Petroleum, Turkey's state oil company, and an additional 5 per cent to Exxon when SOCAR proved unable to come up with the necessary capital.[7] Turkey also has 9 per cent stake in the consortium developing the Shah-Deniz field

Turkey's hopes to have control over flow of early Azeri oil were dashed by the AIOC's refusal of a Turkish proposal in February 1996 to finance the Baku–Batumi pipeline project with very advantageous conditions but under Turkish domination.[8] In November 1997, the 'early' oil from Chirag offshore field in Azerbaijan began to travel to a terminal near Baku, and then via a pipeline crossing southern Russia to the Black Sea port of Novorossisk. As an expert has pointed out, the Azerbaijani policy with respect to its oil reserves has been 'to move ahead on existing projects even before all of the outstanding issues, including those related to legal matters, are resolved'.[9]

Turkmen Gas, Kazak Oil and Turkey

Though not as important as Azeri oil, Turkish foreign-policymakers pay special attention to bringing Turkmen gas to Turkey. Currently Turkey's main gas supplier is Russia, and Ankara aims to add Iran and Turkmenistan to the list to diversify import of this strategic resource. The desperate need for gas in newly industrialized central and eastern Anatolian regions is another motivation for increasing the amount of gas importation.

Turkmenistan consistently backed a plan of laying a Turkmenistan–Turkey–Europe gas pipeline via Iran. In this regard, a decision by the US administration not to hinder realization of the project was highly appreciated in Ashgabat. This pipeline plan was coordinated in 1994 by the interstate council involving Turkmenistan, Iran, Russia, Turkey and Kazakhstan, which was created especially to help build this project. At the same time, international companies, including the Turkish BOTAS, had prepared several routes for laying a pipeline to Turkey, including along the bottom of the Caspian Sea, and via territories of former Soviet republics. The deputy Turkmen Oil and Gas Industry Minister, Gochmurad Nadzhanov, said: 'We, however, are loyal to the understandings reached and back the Iranian version.' He also added that the pipeline's capacity will amount to 28 billion cubic meters of gas a year, out of which 15 billion cubic meters will belong to Turkey, and 13 billion to European countries.[10]

As a concrete step, in February 1996 a joint Turkish–Turkmen group – consisting of the representatives of BOTAS and Turkmen Oil and Gas Ministry – was formed to evaluate options and to reach a decision. According to memorandum of understanding signed between the two countries on 14 February, 'Turkey will purchase 2 billion cubic meters of natural gas in 1998, 5 billion cubic meters between 1999–2004, 10 billion cubic meters between 2005–2009 and 15 billion between 2010–2020.'[11] In December 1996, the Iranian, Turkish and Turkmen oil ministers met in Tehran to discuss the ways of exporting Iranian and Turkmen gas to Turkey. These ministers signed a letter of understanding to meet Ankara's gas needs and transfer of Iranian and Turkmen natural gas to Europe through Turkey. The then Iranian President Hashemi-Rafsanjani received the ministers on 28 December 1996 and stressed the three countries' shared economic concerns and consumption requirements; moreover, he stated that national interests dictate that Iran, Turkey and Turkmenistan cooperate in practice so the gas transfer project can be implemented as rapidly as possible. At the meeting, the Turkish minister, Recai Kutan, repeated Ankara's determination to cooperate toward the construction of a pipeline carrying Turkmen and Iranian gas to European and international markets via Turkish soil. He said that Turkey will carry out such projects decisively in line with its own national interests and regardless of foreign pressure. The Turkmen oil minister, in turn, expressed gratitude for the Islamic Republic of Iran's goodwill and spirit of cooperation, saying his country is ready for the implementation of the project carrying Turkmen and Iranian gas to Europe and international markets via Turkey.[12]

Recai Kutan paid a second visit to Turkmenistan for holding official contacts on petroleum and a natural-gas pipeline in April 1997. During his two-day official visit to Ashgabat, Kutan was received by the Turkmen President Saparmurad Niyazov, the Deputy Prime Minister responsible for oil and gas, the power engineering and industry minister, and the oil and gas minister.[13] Kutan said his visit aimed at bringing natural gas to Turkey from Turkmenistan's rich natural-gas beds and to evaluate other facilities of this country. Kutan said several agreements were signed after his contacts in this country, adding that 'as a result, three billion cubic meters natural gas will be brought to Turkey from Turkmenistan and three billion cubic meters natural gas from Iran will be brought to Turkey'.[14] On 14 May, Niyazov, Rafsanjani and Suleyman Demirel, the leaders of Turkmenistan, Iran and Turkey, respectively, signed a memorandum in Ashgabat on issues concerning the construction of a gas pipeline from Turkmenistan to Europe.[15]

In December 1997, Turkmenistan's President Niyazov and the Turkish Prime Minister Mesut Yilmaz held talks during latter's visit to Ashgabat. They confirmed their intention to build a pipeline from Turkmenistan to

Turkey and legalized a memorandum on mutual understanding to build a Turkmenistan–Turkey–Europe gas pipeline, which was signed by the energy ministers of the two countries. This document formalized for the first time, at the intergovernmental level, a Trans-Caspian project to set up two routes to pump Turkmen gas to the markets of Turkey and Europe. Yilmaz suggested that a possibility should be studied to pump gas from Turkmenistan both on the bottom of the Caspian and then across Azerbaijan and Georgia as well as across the territory of Iran. Niyazov, agreeing in principle with various versions of export pipelines, insisted on recording necessary conditions in the memorandum in order to start work on the Trans-Caspian route.[16]

After all these speculations on various routes and their costs, the French Sofregaz Company presented a feasibility study for the Turkmenistan–Turkey–Europe gas pipeline to the government of Turkmenistan in January 1998. According to the report, the pipeline project envisages two possible routes and several options for the gas transportation. The starting point is the Turkmen gas deposit of Shatlyk. The route will go from the east to the west of Turkmenistan and then continue in parallel with the operating Turkmen–Iranian Korpeje–Kord–Kuy gas pipeline, which was commissioned in December 1997. There are two options for the route in Iran – either along the Caspian coast or to the south of Tehran. Iran is in favor of the latter. If the route goes to the south of Tehran, the construction of the gas pipeline will cost $3.1 billion, if the gas is to be delivered to the Turkish market at Dogubayazit and if the predicted volume of 15 billion cubic meters is recovered. If the route is to be extended to Erzurum, the construction will cost $3.6 billion, and if it is extended to Ankara $4.8 billion.[17] Concerning the Turkmen project, Ashgabat had in mind transiting between 16 and 28 billion cubic meters of gas annually to Turkey and thence to Europe. The Turkish–Turkmen natural gas purchase agreement has been signed in Ashgabat, by the Turkmen State Minister Saparmurat Turkmenbasi and Ziya Aktas, Turkish Energy and Natural Resources Minister, in May 1999.[18] For both projects, the most important challenge will be to find the necessary funds.

Turkey's main ambition related to Kazakhstan is to build an extension to the prospective Baku–Ceyhan pipeline to carry Kazak oil through its territory. Meanwhile, in addition to northern routes, Kazakhstan and the Caspian Pipeline Consortium's (CPC) foreign participants kept alive discussions on alternative projects for pumping Kazakhstani oil for export. In June 1996, an official of the Azerbaijani oil consortium stated that a 'common' Azerbaijani–Georgian or Azerbaijani–Georgian–Turkish route for pumping Caspian oil from Azerbaijan and Kazakhstan had not been ruled out. Back in the autumn of 1995, Kazakhstan and Turkey signed an agreement on the transit of Kazak oil through the Turkish Mediterranean port of Ceyhan. There are two 'stages' regarding this document's implementation – via the Mangyshlak–Baku undersea Trans-Caspian oil pipeline and then via the Azerbaijan–Georgia–Turkey route.[19]

Needless to say, oil was the number-one issue discussed during the Kazakhstani President Nursultan Nazarbayev's visit to Tbilisi and Baku in September 1996. The problem of building export oil pipelines is as important to Tbilisi and Baku as it is to Kazakhstan. According to Nazarbayev, out of a dozen options, two are the most realistic – via Novorossisk or via the Transcaucasus across the Caspian Sea.[20] Kazakhstan's reluctance to transport its oil through Russian land exposed the impact of restrictions on the passage of big tankers through the Bosphorus and Dardanelles Straits.[21] However, if one considers the existence of a pipeline leading to Novorossisk, and Moscow's influential position among the consortium's main investors, the Turkish route is unlikely to be considered in the short or medium term. Kazakhstan prefers the Turkish option in the long term given the fact that by the year 2005 Kazakhstan will need to export up to 25 million tons of oil.[22] In addition, despite Kazakhstan's political support, it would not be possible to build a Trans-Caspian oil pipeline before resolving the legal status problem of the Caspian Sea.

Turkey's Involvement in the Debate Over Pipeline Routes

Further development of Caspian oil reserves will necessitate the establishment of adequate methods by which to transport the oil to consumers in Europe and beyond, and various options are currently under consideration. From the perspective of Azerbaijan and the companies extracting the oil, the factors of principal importance in selecting the optimum route are of course cost, available financing and security. But such business factors alone will not determine the outcome of the debate, as the economic, political and environmental interests of the countries through which the oil would pass have largely come to eclipse such factors.[23]

Before it fully realized the politically charged nature of the debate and the complexity of the factors to take into account, the AIOC consortium initially decided to transport its oil to Western markets via an existing pipeline to the Russian port of Novorossisk, then by tanker through the Black Sea and into the Mediterranean via Turkey's Bosphorus Straits.[24] However, this proposal raised objections from Turkey due to the grave environmental threat posed by the increased shipping volume that this alternative would entail.[25]

Ankara intends to issue a tender for a Vessel Tracking System to facilitate safe passage through the Straits,[26] but no technology can completely eliminate the potential for an oil spill. Some 19 miles long and a mere 700 meters wide at its most narrow point, the Bosphorus is one of the most difficult waterways in the world to navigate, with tankers having to change their course at least 12 times due to abrupt shifts in topography.[27] According to Turkish figures, nearly 45,000 vessels pass through the Straits each year, and there are frequent accidents. The Bosphorus witnessed 167 major accidents in the decade between 1983 and 1993, with the average annual rate of accidents having increased 35 per cent since 1988.[28]

The International Maritime Organization (IMO) warned in 1994 that 'navigation through the Bosphorus Straits ... presents an increasing potential risk to shipping, safety, the environment and the well-being of the local community'.[29] The 1994 *Nassia* tanker accident is an unforgettable example of the threat that shipping poses to the 12 million residents living on both sides of the Bosphorus. In March 1994, the Greek Cypriot tanker *Nassia* collided with another ship, killing 30 seamen and spilling 20,000 tons of oil into the ocean. If this accident had occurred a few miles to the south, Istanbul itself would have faced a major urban disaster.[30]

The Convention of Montreux, adopted in 1936, still regulates the passage of cargo ships through the Bosphorus. It requires the Straits to be kept open to merchant ships of all nations, regardless of the nature of their cargoes. This agreement greatly restricts the ability of the Turkish government to adopt the regulations required to ensure safety of passage through the Bosphorus, but on 1 July 1994, Ankara did what it could under the circumstances when it issued a new set of regulations designed to promote safer traffic. One key objective was the establishment of a traffic separation scheme to maintain safe distance between vessels.[31]

Russia and some other states that border on the Black Sea have complained that Turkey's unilateral interference with shipping in the Straits is illegal – despite the fact that '[f]reedom of passage [required by the Montreux Convention] does not mean uncontrolled passage', as pointed out by the Turkish representative to the IMO.[32]

Following the Turkish government's expression of hesitancy to allow the massive increase in shipping volume that would be involved if the Black Sea route for Azerbaijani oil were used exclusively, the AIOC began to contemplate various alternative routes. One such route would involve transport of oil from Baku to the Turkish port of Ceyhan on the Mediterranean near the Syrian border. [33]

A few other options have also been put forward. The first of these is that of shipping oil from Azerbaijan to the Black Sea port of Poti in Georgia, then on to Odessa in Russia, where the oil would channel into the Druzhba pipeline that extends across Russia and the Ukraine and on to Europe.[34] Gunes Taner, the Turkish Minister of Economy, has proposed yet another alternative called the Novorossisk–Samsun route, which would involve shipping oil by tankers to Turkey's Black Sea port of Samsun and then transporting it south across the Anatolian Peninsula to Ceyhan via a pipeline that would have to be constructed in part. He argued that since there is already a pipeline from Kirikkale – a city in central Turkey – to Ceyhan, the construction costs would be manageable.[35]

The options that have been the subject of the most serious consideration are the Baku–Ceyhan route, and either of the northern routes going through

Russia, with Turkey and Russia each fervently advocating the route passing through their respective territories. Ankara supports the direct Baku–Ceyhan alternative because this route would protect the Bosphorus from the dangers of tanker shipping, still allow Turkey to reap the financial rewards of being a conduit for Caspian oil, and be more direct than the trans-Anatolia alternatives. However, since Turkey has no border with Azerbaijan, a stretch of connecting pipeline through a neighboring country would have to be constructed for the direct Baku-Ceyhan route to be viable.

The shortest route from Azerbaijan to Turkey would be through Armenia. However, ongoing conflict between Armenia and Azerbaijan over Nagorno-Karabakh makes this option unrealistic for the near future for security reasons. The US government objects to the transport of oil through Iranian territory pursuant to its general policy of limiting the international trade and investment prospects for the fundamentalist republic. This factor seriously diminishes the likelihood that this alternative will be chosen. Recently, the White House announced that it would not oppose transportation of oil from Turkmenistan through Iran to Turkey,[36] which can be taken as an indication that the Iranian route through Azerbaijan is not out of the question after all. But until Washington actually gives the nod, its acquiescence cannot be counted on.

If US resistance to the Iranian route remains strong, the only alternative for the transport of Azerbaijani oil into Turkey would be through Georgia, in a deviation from the Novorossisk–Samsun route proposed by Gunes Taner. Again, this route would take the oil from fields in Azerbaijan to Georgian ports, and from there by tanker to Turkish ports on the Black Sea, then by pipeline across Turkey to Ceyhan.[37] Another Georgian option is a route from Baku directly across Georgia, then down through Turkey to Ceyhan, thus bypassing the Black Sea altogether. The length of the pipeline from the Georgian border to Ceyhan would be about 1,900 kilometers, and the cost of construction of the pipeline would be an estimated $3 billion. The Turkish government has declared that it is ready to finance the entire cost of any pipeline that would pass through its territory.[38] Turkey's President Suleyman Demirel and the Georgian leader Eduard Shevardnadze expressed their joint support for a route through Georgia during a visit by Demirel to Tbilisi in November 1994.[39]

Ankara is quick to point out that Ceyhan can handle many times the capacity of the Russian port of Novorossisk. In addition, Ceyhan is open all year due to the calm climate of the Mediterranean, whereas Black Sea ports are shut down in the winter by dangerous weather conditions.[40] As expressed by Ahat Andican, a state minister and an influential figure in shaping Turkish policy toward the Turkic republics of the former Soviet Union, 'the total output from the Caspian and Central Asia will eventually be 50 to 60 million tons a year, but the Baku–Novorossisk and Baku–Supsa routes have a combined capacity of 16 million tons [a year]. Therefore the Baku–Ceyhan pipeline is the most inevitable and stable option.'[41]

Some critics of the Baku-Ceyhan route have attempted to bring the Kurdish insurrection in eastern Turkey to the forefront of the debate, portraying it as a potential threat to the security of the pipeline. By the end of 1997, this argument seemed to lose its force, given that the Turkish army and security forces began to have considerable success in suppressing Kurdish military activity.[42]

Turkey is far from alone in its advocacy for the Baku–Ceyhan route. The former president of the AIOC, Terry Adams, has thrown his weight behind this proposal as well. Jim Norosky, vice-president of the US company Amoco (which holds a 17.01 per cent stake in the AIOC), has also suggested that the Baku–Ceyhan route is preferable, despite the extra cost imposed by its greater length. Such extra cost, he suggests, should be offset by tax breaks or other measures on the part of the relevant authorities.[44] Turkey has also succeeded in gaining the support of the Azerbaijani President Heydar Aliyev, who has stated that he is in favor of giving priority to the direct Baku–Ceyhan alternative. He expressed this position during a visit to Turkey, and then later during a visit to the United States.[45] In March 1998, a meeting of the foreign ministers of Azerbaijan, Turkey, Georgia, Kazakhstan and Turkmenistan was held in Turkey with the participation of the president of the AIOC. The primary purpose of the meeting was to brief the four other countries about the work that is under way on the feasibility of the Baku–Ceyhan pipeline, and these states confirmed their support for project. The foreign ministers of Russia and Iran were not invited to Istanbul for the meeting, thus prompting Russia to officially express its 'legitimate bewilderment' over the events.[46]

At this point the most significant obstacle that Turkey faces in its efforts to establish the Baku–Ceyhan pipeline is Russian opposition. Russia has a deep fear that, if any route for transporting Azerbaijani oil bypasses Russian territory, Russia will not only lose a lucrative source of revenue but will also experience the diminishing of its economic and political influence in this resource-rich region.[47] It is for this reason that the Turkish decision to restrict tanker passage on the Bosphorus was received so bitterly by Russia.

IRAN AND RUSSIA: STANDING BETWEEN TURKEY AND THE CASPIAN RICHES

Iran: The Pragmatic Radical

Iran is one of the most prominent players in the Azerbaijani oil controversy and a principal obstacle to Azerbaijan's ambition of becoming one of the world's great energy producers. Given that Turkey hopes to continue to play a significant role in the extraction of Azerbaijan's oil reserves through participation in international consortia, and expects to become host to at least one

15

of the pipelines that will carry oil to the West, Turkey's interests in the resolution of the dispute over the Caspian's legal status are closely aligned with those of Azerbaijan. For this reason the Caspian policy of Iran is watched closely not only by Azerbaijan but also by Turkey.

Iran's policy with respect to the Caspian is currently characterized by a marked hostility to investment in the region by Western businesses. For example, Ali Akbar Nateq-Nouri, the speaker of Iran's parliament, was recently quoted as saying that the United States should be restricted from participating in Caspian ventures since any involvement by US companies would simply represent an effort by the US government to satisfy its 'historical dream' of establishing influence in the region.[48] Nateq-Nouri added that Azerbaijan's President Aliyev is 'making a historic mistake by laying grounds for US interference'.[49] In August 1997, Iran's Vice-President Mahmoud Vaezi stated that 'certain states have caused unrest in the sensitive region by signing unilateral contracts with foreign companies'.[50] Vaezi did not mention Azerbaijan by name, though it was obvious that it was the target of the barb due to its demonstrated willingness to do business with Westerners.

One might conclude from such heated expressions of disapproval of Western participation that Iran's Caspian policy has been dictated by ideology, and rather predictably so, given Iran's general hostility toward the West, rooted in fundamentalism, since the 1979 Revolution. However, such an interpretation of events is flawed: on the whole, Iran's Caspian policy has been decidedly pragmatic and driven by economic concerns.

When the idea of joint Western and Central Asian oil ventures was first proposed, Iran demonstrated approval – or at least acquiescence – and expressed a willingness to participate in any such venture. Indeed, Iran sought to obtain a 5 per cent share in the AIOC consortium called for under the 'Contract of the Century'. However, Tehran quickly saw this ambition frustrated by US pressure to exclude Iranian interests.[51] The official excuse put forward was that US law forbids American companies from doing business with Iranian companies, and so the American interests that were already part of the consortium would have to pull out if Iranian participation were allowed.[52] So it was the West that sought to exclude Iran from the divvying up of profits, rather than vice versa. It is this event, this inflicting of an economic wound, that one can identify as the trigger of Iran's vocal opposition to Western investment activity in the Caspian.

Iran's position with regard to the legal status of the Caspian is also indicative of its pragmatic, economics-oriented approach. Tehran has sided with Russia in its former stance that the Caspian is a 'lake' rather than a 'sea'. If the former classification is ultimately agreed upon and the water body's resources are divided up communally rather than territorially, Tehran stands to gain a much larger share of the Caspian pie than it would under the alternative arrangement.[53]

The fact that Iran and Russia both stand to benefit from the 'lake' classification has provided an incentive for Iran to align its overall regional policy with that of Russia where possible, so as to create an atmosphere of solidarity and cooperation between the two countries. Thus, for example, Iran joined Russia in support of Armenia in its conflict with Azerbaijan over Nagorno-Karabakh.[54] This is solid evidence that the Islamic Republic's Caspian policy is dictated by pragmatism rather than ideology. Other evidence of the growing alignment between these two powers includes a series of arms sales by Russia to Iran, and an avowed shared desire to see a change of leadership in Afghanistan.[55]

In contrast, relations between Iran and Azerbaijan have been worsening over the last few years. Iran's act of siding with Azerbaijan's enemy on the Nagorno-Karabakh issue is only one manifestation of the ill will between these neighbors. Another came in 1995, when Iran virtually closed its border with Azerbaijan and temporarily cut off electricity to Nakhichevan – an autonomous Azeri enclave dependent on Iranian power.[56]

The breakdown in relations apparently stems from three factors. First is the obvious fact that Azerbaijan has as of yet refused to accept the Russian–Iranian position with regard to the legal status of the Caspian. Second is Azerbaijan's eagerness to do business with Western companies despite the exclusion of Iran, as demonstrated by Azerbaijan's continued blessing of the AIOC deal. Third is Iran's fear that a prosperous, independent Azerbaijan would be an unwelcome role model to the enormous Azeri minority that makes up a quarter of Iran's population, and which constitutes a majority in several northern Iranian provinces.[57] Iran surely fears that increased affluence and international strategic clout will embolden tiny Azerbaijan and give it the courage to incite nationalistic sentiment in its ethnic brethren across the border.

Azerbaijan has made some efforts to placate Tehran, as when it granted Iran a 10 per cent share in a separate oil venture to develop fields in the Shah–Deniz area[58] – a move that Baku was able to manage without unduly raising the ire of Washington because no American companies were involved in the Shah–Deniz deal, and thus no violation of US law would follow from Iranian participation. However, such efforts have not brought about much of a thawing of relations between the two neighbors.

Russia: Government Policy at Odds with Industry Prerogatives

This former world superpower faced the humiliation of losing its historical possessions early in the last decade, but is beginning to have something of an economic resurgence and seems to be flirting with the notion of re-embracing its old imperialist ways on a regional scale.

Not satisfied with presenting legal arguments at regional and international fora in support of its call for communal division of Caspian resources, Russia has also reportedly attempted to force the outcome by direct interference in domestic politics of the Caspian states. According to *The Economist*, Russia has 'left its fingerprints on one or two past attempts to unseat Azerbaijan's president, Heydar Aliyev',[59] who has stood unwavering in his resistance to anything but a strictly territorial division of the Caspian.

Russia has also amassed troops on its Caucasian borders in excess of the limits established by the 1990 Conventional Forces in Europe treaty (CFE), asserting that Russia's current security needs require an even greater presence in the region than was necessary during the Soviet period.[60] Russia previously expressed the desire to increase its forces in the area to an amount well over the threshold set by the CFE.[61]

While events in the last few years in Chechnya and Nagorno-Karabakh suggest that Russia is not unreasonable in recognizing a security concern in the Caucasus, it is not unlikely that Russia has overstated the concern and is attempting to use its still-formidable military might to intimidate its recalcitrant former possession to the south into ending its resistance to Russian ambitions in the Caspian. Indeed, Moscow has not tried to hide that it is keeping the option of military intervention open; Russia stated in the document sent to the United Nations that it 'reserves the right to take necessary steps at any time that it considers appropriate in order to restore law and order and liquidate the consequences of unilateral actions'[62] on the part of any of the littoral states with regard to the Caspian's energy reserves.

Russia has also been accused by Azerbaijan of feeding the ongoing conflict over Nagorno-Karabakh by transferring large amounts of sophisticated weaponry to Armenia free of charge.[63] Russian Defense Minister Rodionov admitted the facts of this affair in 1997. Again, such weapons transfers may be a method of intimidation designed to bring Azerbaijan into line.

Yet another example of Russian pressure on Azerbaijan was its act of closing the two countries' only land border in 1995 – a move that virtually cut off trade between Azerbaijan and Russia.[64] Moscow's aggressive posture toward Azerbaijan, while obviously motivated by a desire to increase Russia's economic opportunities in the Caspian, may end up hurting Russian economic interests in the long run. If ill will prevails between the two countries, Russian oil interests will likely be excluded from participation in future ventures to develop Azerbaijani deposits. Indeed, Russia's relentless efforts to guarantee a larger share of Caspian output has already cost the principal Russian private oil companies one major deal in Azerbaijan. This occurred in August 1997, when the Russian government forced the cancellation of a contract signed by the LUKoil and Rosneft companies, forcing them to renounce participation in an international consortium organized to develop the Kyapaz offshore oilfield.[65] The Kyapaz field is claimed by Turkmenistan, which views its exploitation under Azerbaijani supervision as an illegitimate appropriation. Accordingly, in making this calculated move Russia was hoping to win

Turkmen favor and draw that country over to its side as an advocate for Moscow's policy toward Caspian. In addition, Russia's upper hand in Caspian Pipeline Consortium (CPC) – the body charged with constructing an export pipeline from Kazakhstan's giant Tengiz oilfield – is the primary obstacle to Turkey's plans to transport Kazak oil through Turkish territory.

But, even beyond problems with Azerbaijan, Kazakhstan and Turkmenistan, Russia's aggressive policy runs the risk of alienating other countries in the region who may view Russia's efforts as a return to its old imperial ways. Without goodwill and amiable relations with the newly independent countries of Central Asia and the Transcaucasus, they are less likely to encourage the development of stronger trade ties with Russia or to promote Russian investment in their economies by offering tax breaks and other incentives. Indeed, they may even put up barriers to Russian investment, as long as alternative sources of technology and capital are forthcoming. These new republics are likely to be pushed farther from their historic trading partner to the north, into the increasingly eager embraces of the capital-rich West and an ever more developed Turkey, or even pressed into closer affiliation with Islamic Iran.

There is growing evidence that private oil interests in Russia are becoming disenchanted with Moscow's strong-arm approach to the Caspian dispute. Upon being forced out of the Kyapaz consortium by the Kremlin, a LUKoil representative reportedly expressed 'bewilderment' over the move.[66] Moreover, oil interests seem mindful of the risk of alienating other new republics south of Russia's borders. As related by Yuri Federov, 'the oil people want to respect national aspirations of other new independent states, while at the same time expecting that those states would decide to make maximum use of the scientific, technological, human potential still possessed by Russia'.[67] Respect for national autonomy in exchange for government facilitation of economic relations seems to be shared only nominally by the Kremlin at this point, and it is the private sector in Russia that stands to lose from this posture.

While Russian businesses may suffer in the long run from their government's Caspian policy, Turkey may well stand to gain from it. Turkey has already benefited from the development of Azerbaijani oil reserves, as the state-run Turkish oil company, TPAO, received a 6.75 per cent stake in the consortium developing the Azeri, Chirag and Guneshli oilfields and a 9 per cent stake in the consortium developing the Shah–Deniz field. Moreover, any shares in future projects that would have gone to Russia but for Moscow's alienation of Azerbaijan may be picked up at least in part by Turkish entities.

Even apart from participation in the direct exploitation of oil deposits, Turkey would benefit from Azerbaijani enmity toward Russia when it comes to the making of a final determination on the pipeline route for the transport of Azerbaijani oil to the West. As mentioned above, prominent figures in the

AIOC (which is highly responsive to the dictates of the Azerbaijani government due to the large profit share of the state oil company and the AIOC's dependence on official recognition for its very legal existence) have recently expressed tentative approval of the Baku–Ceyhan route through Turkey.

Finally, the more alienated from Russia that Azerbaijan and the other new republics of the region become, the more likely they will be to seek out the support of Ankara and to elicit Turkish participation in their economies. Indeed, Turkish companies have already set up operations in Azerbaijan, including such industrial giants as TPAO, Bayraktar Holding, Koç's Ram Division and Borusan Makina's Caterpillar Division, not to mention many smaller firms.[68] Interestingly, the political problems discussed above could not prevent Turco-Russian trade to the tune of several billion dollars, and economic relations seem likely to grow further.

TURKEY AND THE UNITED STATES: A TALE OF TWO ALLIES

From Turkey's perspective, its long-time ally the United States has the potential to play a very constructive role in the region as a counterweight to the ambitions of Russia and Iran and as an advocate of Turkish interests. The 'Turkish knocking' on the American door has been successful. Ankara has been trying to become an effective element on the energy map in Central Asia and the primary geostrategic player in the Turkish-speaking world in cooperation with Israel. The effectiveness of any US efforts in this regard will be commensurate with the extent to which Washington can manage to avoid raising nationalistic ire in Russia when promoting Turkish interests and contribute to stability and prosperity in Azerbaijan, the country that is the key to Turkish oil ambitions.

Some nationalist-minded individuals influential in Russian foreign policy view the prospect of any US influence within the territory once controlled by the Soviet Union as a security challenge and have proposed serious measures to resist it. A Russian military expert, Anton Surikov, is one such figure; he has argued that 'we are witnessing US intensive efforts to create a sanitary cordon around Russia in Ukraine, Georgia, Azerbaijan and the Central Asian states. The euphemism for this plan is creating a so-called "Eurasian transport corridor." Our duty is to counteract these plans'.[69] The US government will have to tread carefully if it is to avoid doing anything Russian nationalists could misconstrue as aggressive and point to in their efforts to raise the bristles of those who wield power in the Russian government and military.

Every effort should be made to convey the image that the players in the oil controversies are not involved in a zero-sum game. In other words, everyone will win in the long run if cooperation and moderation prevail. But Washington should not be so timid in response to Russian blustering that

American businesses will be denied the opportunity to share in the profits to be reaped in the Caspian, and so that Russia will gain exclusive control over the distribution of Azerbaijani oil. Such a development would allow Russia not only to price gouge on a day-to-day basis but even to hold potential consumers of Azerbaijani oil hostage if an oil crisis like those that occurred in the 1970s and early 1980s should ever again arise. A country like Turkey, which is expected to become increasingly dependent on fuel imports in the coming decades, would be particularly vulnerable to such maneuvers.

Aware of the threat that Russian monopolization of oil transport would pose, the then-US Energy Secretary Federico Peña stated in mid-1997 that the US supports 'the concept of multiple pipelines and multiple pipeline routes through the region as oil and gas are extracted'.[70] Washington has advocated the selection of the Baku–Ceyhan pipeline route, among others, in tune with its multiple pipeline policy. Indeed, President Clinton personally lobbied Azerbaijan's President Aliyev to consider the Turkish pipeline.[71] Such advocacy of the Turkish position is a prudent one for Washington, as the Baku–Ceyhan route is not only likely to prove viable and secure but should also bring significant revenues to Turkey to finance future development projects. From Washington's perspective, this is in the interests of American foreign policy, because a strong Turkey represents a positive, secular model for the newly independent Turkic republics of the region who are always being courted by fundamentalist Iran. Yet Clinton also wisely encouraged Aliyev to consider the northern route through Russia *in addition to* the Turkish route,[72] a move that was calculated to avoid the appearance that Washington stands in opposition to Russian interests. In April 1999, Aliyev told Jan Kalicki (the US President's coordinator of cooperation with CIS member-states in energy and trade) that the construction of the main export pipeline delivering the bulk of Caspian oil from Baku to Ceyhan, Turkey, will start in the near future.[73]

A second way that the United States can further Turkey's interests is to lend greater support to Azerbaijan than it has previously offered. Such efforts would not simply represent gratuitous favors to Turkey, but would be in the interest of American oil companies given that Azerbaijan has demonstrated consistent eagerness to deal with Western businesses even in the face of stolid opposition from Russia and Iran – two powerful neighbors with a presence much more tangible than that of the United States in the Caspian region.

The first step that Washington should take in this direction is to lift Section 907, a provision of US law enacted in 1992 as part of the Freedom Support Act. Section 907 forbids direct US government aid to the government of Azerbaijan, including humanitarian assistance.[74] It was passed by the US Congress at the insistence of a powerful Armenian lobby, and it has been the continued advocacy of this group that has kept it in place. According to the *Washington Post*, Section 907 'was enacted over the opposition of the Bush administration and now is opposed by the Clinton administration'.[75] At this point Armenia clearly has the upper hand in the conflict between the two countries, considering that it still holds 20 per cent of Azerbaijan's territory,[76] and so the concern over aggression against Armenia or ethnic Armenians in Nagorno-Karabakh that was used to justify the measure now lacks foundation. The lifting of Section 907 would allow Washington to provide a much-needed infusion of funds to this impoverished nation.

The movement to scrap Section 907 seems to be picking up speed. US Congressman Lee Hamilton (D – Indiana) recently argued that 'Congress should lift the ban on Azerbaijan to give us maximum leverage on behalf of peace. A better relationship with Azerbaijan serves the U.S. national interest, the interest of peace, and the long-term interests of Armenia as well'.[78] In addition, this will also strengthen Turkey's hand in the Caspian controversies.

CONCLUSION

The staggering magnitude of Caspian hydrocarbon deposits presents the potential for a tremendous economic boom for each of the five littoral states, as well as for those states – such as Turkey – that hope to benefit directly from them. The discovery of resources on such a terrific scale offers the potential for every one of these nations to increase its overall level of economic development, raise the standard of living of its population, and carry itself into the twenty-first century with a new-found strategic importance and inter-national prestige. One may object that the fall of oil prices, since second half of 1998, restricted the prospect, but it goes almost without saying that the possible oil revenue, at any condition, promises much to the development of the littoral states and will continue to attract regional countries. Yet mutual enmity and distrust have stemmed from controversies born from this fabulous potential, and such bitter emotions have eclipsed the excitement and optimism that it should have inspired. Indeed, neighbors that stand only to gain from their fortuitous proximity to such rich deposits are faced with the prospect of economic blockades, severed diplomatic relations or even military clashes in this region. The last prospect is one that threatens not only those with a direct stake in the controversies but also their allies and those unfortunate disinter-ested countries that might suffer the spillover of refugees or other side effects of war merely because of their location on the map.

Given these facts, each of the countries with a stake in the Caspian con-troversies should strive to maintain at all times an atmosphere of cooperation, patience and goodwill. The respective governments should do their utmost to maintain the lines of communication through elaborate diplomatic channels and regular regional and international conferences, and should move slowly and avoid any unilateral action that could be perceived as an attempt to pre-empt resolution of these debates.

As for the debate over the legal status of the Caspian, Russia and Iran need to recognize the enormous stake that Azerbaijan has in its outcome. As a positive development, Moscow began to give signals of compromise in this regard. From the perspective of Azerbaijan, something approaching an equal distribution of the Caspian's resources would mean giving up its ambitions of becoming a player in world energy markets and of making a pervasive impact on its backward economy. While revenue from the Caspian's exploitation would be substantial even to such large powers as Iran and Russia, their futures will not be made or broken over the outcome of this issue.

As for the other major controversy, the principal rivals in the dispute over pipeline routing – Russia and Turkey – should accept the notion that *both* can play host to pipelines to transport Azerbaijani oil. Yet, in the short term, Russia must come to terms with the fact that, without an affirmative effort on the part of the Kremlin, the Russian private sector and international capital interests in addressing the deficiencies of the northern pipeline network, Russia cannot safely be a conduit for the huge volume of oil that increased exploitation of the Caspian will entail. Russia may have to step aside for the time being and devote itself to developing its carrying capacity, rather than alienate all of its neighbors with aggressive behavior. It may well prove to be the case that once Russia concedes that the northern route will not be the exclusive avenue for Caspian oil, and turns its attention to developing a modern pipeline network, the financing will materialize and the wait will be shorter than currently expected.

The consistent US support and the approval of the Turkic Caspian states increased the likelihood of the implementation of the Baku–Ceyhan project. Turkish foreign policy makers should go steady on the implementation of this project and should not propose any other option. It should be noted that, even after the AIOC's probable decision to choose Baku–Ceyhan as the major pipeline route (or one of them), such a decision will not mean that Azeri oil will flow through Turkish territory. There will still be many more obstacles for Ankara to cross before realizing its ambitions in the Caspian region. In case of the AIOC's refusal of the Baku–Ceyhan option, it should be kept in mind that this project will continue to have potential for the rest of Caspian oil.[79] Another important factor that Turkish authorities should keep in mind is the need to make necessary revisions in the existing legal system to attract private investment. Under current regulations, state monopoly restricts entrance of private firms to the related industries, e.g. pipeline construction.

The key for Russia, Azerbaijan, Turkey and each of the other states with a stake in the outcome of these controversies is to view one another as a partner rather than a rival and to realize that, when another country among them benefits from an economic opportunity and furthers its prosperity, this does not represent a loss to the others. Rather, the domestic stability that prosperity on the part of one country facilitates will ensure every other country in the region the opportunity to develop and prosper in its own right, free from the threat of opportunistic aggression.

NOTES

1. For detailed information on new developments in Turkish foreign policy, see Kemal Kirisci, 'New Patterns of Turkish Foreign Policy Behavior', in Cigdem Balim, Ersin Kalaycioglu and Gareth Winrow (eds), *Turkey: Political, Social, and Economic Challenges in the 1990s* (Leiden: E.J. Brill, 1995).
2. Temel Iskit, 'Turkey: A New Actor in the Field of Energy Politics', Perceptions 1, No. 1 (March–May 1996), p.66.
3. Ibid., p.71.
4. 'Armenia/Azerbaijan: Tensions Renewed in Nagorno-Karabakh', *Periscope Daily Defense News Capsules* (26 June 1997).
5. Roman Rollnick, 'Controversy Over Oil Pipeline in the Caspian Region', *Earth Times News Service*, 27 August 1997, via Habarlar-L: Azerbaijan News Distribution List, Habarlar-L-Request@USC.edu; Vladimir Misin, 'Skolko nefti vi Azerbayjana?', (How much Oil in Azerbaijan?), Neft i Kapital (Moscow) No. 2 (February 1995), p.50.
6. Andrei Shoumikhin, 'Economics and Politics of Developing Caspian Oil Resources', *Perspectives on Central Asia* (November 1996), http://www.cpss.org/casianw/novpers.html.
7. Rosemarie Forstythe, *The Politics of Oil in the Caucasus and Central Asia*, Adelphi Papers, No. 40 (Oxford: International Institute for Strategic Studies, 1996, pp.40–1.
8. Suha Bolukbasi, 'The Controversy Over the Caspian Sea Mineral Resources: Conflicting Perceptions, Clashing Interests', *Europe-Asia Studies* 50, No. 3 (May 1998), pp.405–6.
9. Andrei Shoumikhin, 'New Developments Related to Caspian Oil', *Perspectives on Central Asia* (December 1996), http://www.cpss.org/casianw/canews.htm; 'Novaya neftyanaya otrasi Kaspiya' (Caspian's New Oil Industry), *Neftegazovay Vertical*, No .5 (1998), pp.100–3; Aleksey Comov, 'Neftnovogo veka' (Oil of New Century), *Neft Rossii*, No. 10 (1997), p.5.
10. Interfax, 14 March 1996, in Foreign Broadcast Information Service – Central Eurasia (hereafter FBIS-SOV), #96–052, 18 March 1996.
11. *Turkish Daily News*, 16 February 1996.
12. *Voice of the Islamic Republic of Iran First Program Network*, 28 December 1996, in Foreign Broadcast Information Service – Near East and South Asia (hereafter FBIS-NES), #96–251, 7 January 1997.
13. *Anatolia*, 28 April 1997.
14. Ibid., 1 May 1997.
15. Mayak Radio Network in Russian, 14 May 97, in FBIS-SOV, #97–134, 15 May 1997.
16. ITAR-TASS, 28 December 1997, in FBIS-SOV, #97–362, 1 January 1998.
17. ITAR-TASS, 30 January 1998, in FBIS-SOV, #98–030, 4 February 1998.
18. *Anatolia*, 21 May 1999.
19. *Rossiyskaya Gazeta*, 22 June 1996, in FBIS-SOV, #96–124, 27 June 1996.
20. A. Auken, R. Julamanov, *Nefti gaz Kazakhistana* (Kazak Oil and Gas), Institute Razvitiya Kazakistana (Almati), (1995), p.8.
21. Interfax, 19 May 97, in FBIS-SOV, #97–139, 22 June 1997.
22. V. Aleksandrov, 'Neft iz Tengiza: proekt 21. veka' (Oil from Tengiz: Project of 21st Century), *Mejdunarodnaya Jizn*, No. 5 (1998), p.93; Radio Rossii Network, 10 September 1997, in FBIS-SOV, #97–253, 12 September 1997.
23. Oumerserik Kasenov, 'Russia, Transcaucasia, and Central Asia: Oil, Pipelines, and Geopolitics', in Roald Z. Sagdeev and Susan Eisenhower (eds.), *Central Asia: Conflict, Resolution, and Change* (Chevy Chase: CPSS Press, 1997), p.78.
24. 'Pipeline Stakes', *Washington Post*, 30 October 1995, p.A16.
25. 'Great Game is Afoot Again as Rivals Carve Up Oil Bonanza', *Independent* (London), 21 May 1997; for Russian view see, Oleg Maksimov, 'Novi Neftyanov paradok neminuta privedit k geopolitisciskim izmeneniem' (New Oil Order will Bring Inevitable Geopolitical Changes), *Sodrujetva N.G.*, No. 10 (November 1998), p.1.

26. Terence Adams and Gregory Rich, 'Great Power Politics and the Azerbaijan Oil Pipeline', *Washington Institute of Near East Policy: Policy Watch* (24 February 1997), http://www.washingtoninstitute.org/watch/Policywatch/policywatch1997/237.htm.
27. Michael Rank, 'Russia and Turkey Clash Over Control of Bosphorus', Reuters, 25 July 1997.
28. 'The Bosphorus: A Waterway at Risk', via the web page of the Turkish Ministry of Foreign Affairs, http://www.mfa.gov.tr/grupf/caspian3.htm.
29. Ibid.
30. 'Accidents in the Bosphorus', via the web page of the Turkish Ministry of Foreign Affairs, http://www.mfa.gov.tr/grupf/caspian5.htm.
31. Ozlem Topses, 'Turkish Regulations Regarding Maritime Traffic in the Turkish Straits and Sea of Marmara', via the web page of the Turkish Ministry of Foreign Affairs, http://www.mfa.gov.tr/grupi/ maritime.htm.
32. Rank, 'Russia and Turkey Clash'. While Russian authorities oppose Turkey's objections taking environmental issues into consideration, they do not hesitate to raise the same kinds of objections related to the exploitation of the Caspian Sea Basin. For further information see, G. M. Abdurahmanov, 'Puti obespeceneniya ustoyaivogo razvitiya sosiyoprirodnogo kompleksa prikaspiyskogo basseyna' (Providing natural development of Caspian region), *Problemi ekologiceskoy bezopasnosti Kaspiyskogo regiona*, Moscow-Mahackale 1997; D. R. Aliyev, 'Ekonomiceskoye i sosialno-ekologiceskoye razvitiye Dagestana v svyazi s problemami Kaspiya' (Daghestan's economic and environmental developments related to Caspian), *Buduseye Dagestana*, Mahackala 1994; P. A. Adayeva, 'Otsenka ekologiceskogo sostoyaniya ekosistemi Kaspiyskogo morya' (Analysis of the ecological system of Caspian Sea), *Materiali 14 naucno-prakticeskoy konferntsiyi po ohrane prirodi Dagestana*, Mohackala 1997; A. A. Gadjiyev, U. V. Novikov, M. M. Sayfutdinov, *Ohrana okrujayusey sredi v Dagestana* (Protecting Daghestan's natural environment), Mahackala, 1987; B. V. Yerofeyev, *Ekologiceskoye pravo* (Law of environment), Moscow 1998; N. M. Mirzoyeva, 'O probleme neftyanih zagryazneniy okrujayusey prirodnoy sredi' (Problems of oil pollution in environment), *Ekologiceskiy Vestnik 3*, Mahackala 1998.
33. Iskit, 'Turkey: A New Actor', p.70.
34. Georgy Dvali, 'Tbilisi is Pleased with Aliyev's Visit to Ukraine', *Kommersant Daily*, 27 March 1997, in *The Current Digest of Post-Soviet Press*, No. 25 (1997), p.49.
35. Ozlem Hersan, 'Taner'den Petrole Alternatif', *Yeni Yuzyil*, 28 August 1997, p.8.
36. Patricia Kranz, 'Look What's Bubbling Up in the Caspian', *Business Week*, 15 September 1997, p.21.
37. Kasenov, 'Russia, Transcaucasia, and Central Asia', p.71.
38. Ibid.
39. Elizabeth Fuller, 'The Caspian Pipeline Tug of War', *Open Media Research Institute Program Brief*, 3 October 1995.
40. Alexei Baliyev, 'The Caspian Sea: Nobody Safe in the Eye of the Storm', *Rossiskaya Gazeta*, 18 July 1997, cited in Turkestan Newsletter, No. 97, 28 July 1997; and Iskit, 'Turkey: A New Actor', p.65.
41. Ercan Ersoy, 'Turkey to Lobby for Baku–Ceyhan Pipeline', Reuters, 21August 1997.
42. See Umit Ozdag, 'Kuzey Irak ve PKK', *Avrasya Dosyasi 3*, No. 1 (Spring), pp.27–30.
43. Iskit, 'Turkey: A New Actor', p.79.
44. Gulnara Achilova, 'Crude Oil to Take Three Routes', *Nezavisimaya Gazeta*, 17 June 1997, in *The Current Digest of the Post-Soviet Press*, No .19 (1997), p.49.
45. Reuters, 14 July 1997.
46. Interfax, 3 March 1998.
47. Kasenov, 'Russia, Transcaucasia, and Central Asia', p.68.
48. 'Iranian Leader Blames U.S. for Stoking Caspian Row', Reuters World Service, 12 April 1997.
49. Ibid.
50. Michael S. Lelyveld, 'Give Us a Piece of the Action', *Journal of Commerce*, 8 August 1997, p.3A.
51. Marshall Ingewerson, 'The Next Great Game: Players Jostle to Pipe Home a Share of the Oil Prize', *Christian Science Monitor*, 25 August 1997, p.10.
52 Ibid.
53. Shoumikhin, 'New Developments Related to Caspian Oil'.

54. Ingewerson, 'The Next Great Game', p.57.
55. 'The Caucasus: Azerbaijan', *APS Diplomat Strategic Balance in the Middle East*, 2 October 1995.
56. Ingewerson, 'The Next great Game', p.57.
57. Ibid.
58. Ibid.
59. 'The Combustible Caspian', *Economist*, 11 January 1997, p.45.
60. Odile Meuvret, 'Russia Scuppers Conventional Arms Limitation Talks', Agence France Presse, 16 November 1995.
61. Brooks Tigner, 'Force Levels Hike Turk, Russian Friction', *Defense News*, 26 November 1995, p.4.
62. Kasenov, 'Russia, Transcaucasia, and Central Asia', p.69.
63. 'Armenia/Azerbaijan'.
64. 'Consortium to Develop Caspian Sea Oil Fields', *The Herald* (Glasgow), 9 October 1995, p.16; Oleg Maksimov, 'Novi Neftyanov paradok neminuta privedit k geopolitisciskim izmeneniem' (New Oil Order will Bring Inevitable Geopolitical Changes), *Sodrujetva N.G.*, No. 10, (November 1998), p.1.
65. Lycedmila Romanova, 'Intersi neftyanoy diplomatii' (Interests of Oil Diplomacy), *Sadrujestvo N.G.*, No. 2 (February 1999) p.13; 'Turkmenistan to Launch International Oil, Gas Tender Monday', Agence France Presse, 30 August 1997.
66. A. M. Butayev, *Kaspiyi more ili ozero?* (Is Caspian a sea or lake?), Mahackala, 1998; 'Turkmen–Azeri Oilfield Dispute Remains Unresolved', BBC Summary of World Broadcasts, 8 August 1997.
67. Yuri Federov, 'Russia's Policies Toward Caspian Region Oil: Neo Imperial or Pragmatic II?', *Perspectives on Central Asia* (October 1996), http://www.cpss.org/casianw/octpers.html.
68. Michael Kuser, 'The Great Chess Match', *Turkish Daily News*, 15 August 1997.
69. V. Semyonov, 'Manageable Chaos', *Zavtra*, 19 May 1997, via Russian Press Electronic Courier, 17 June 1997; sasha@solar.rtd.utk.edu.
70. 'U.S. Wants Multiple Caspian Oil Pipeline Routes', Reuters, 23 July 1997.
71. 'Pipeline Stakes'; Semen Novoprudskiy, 'Amerika sivyazi-vaet Turkmenistan i Turciyu' (America is Connecting Turkey and Turkmenistan), *Finansovie Izvestiya*, No. 7 (February 1999), p.6.
72. Ibid.
73. Interfax, 20 April 1999, in FBIS-SOV, #99–0420, 21 April 1998.
74. 'United States assistance under this or any other Act (other than assistance under title V of this Act) may not be provided to the Government of Azerbaijan until the President determines, and so reports to the Congress, that the Government of Azerbaijan is taking demonstrable steps to cease all blockades and other offensive uses of force against Armenia and Nagorno-Karabakh.' Freedom for Russia and Emerging Eurasian Democracies and Open Markets Support Act of 1992 (Freedom Support Act). US Public Law 102–511, 102d Cong., 3rd sess., 24 October 1992.
75. 'Oil and Turmoil in the Caucasus', *Washington Post*, 19 July 1997.
76. 'Armenia/Azerbaijan'.
77. Micheal P. Croissant, 'ABD'nin Trans-Kafkasya Politikasi' (America`s Transcaucasian Policy), *Zaman*, 1 September 1998, p.6.
78. Lee H. Hamilton, 'Toward Peace in the Caucasus', *Christian Science Monitor*, 23 July 1997.
79. For a pessimistic view on the Baku–Ceyhan project see, Kenan Guluzade, 'Baku–Djeyhan pora li pisat nekrolog?' (Time to Say Goodbye to Baku–Ceyhan?), *Nefti Gaz Kaspiya* (Moscow), No. 1 (1998), pp.121–2; V. Anrianov, 'Velikiy neftyanov put nameste velikogo selkovogo' (Oil road instead of Silk Route), *Neft Rossii*, No. 1 (1998), p.25.

2

GREECE'S SECURITY DILEMMA IN THE CAUCASUS

Greece's activity in the Caucasus has expanded greatly since 1994. Greek policy-makers have been active at building ties with all three regional states – Armenia, Azerbaijan and Georgia. Although Greece's activities may be viewed in terms of the bilateral relations it has established with each of the Caucasus republics, they are best viewed in the context of wider geopolitical developments.

The Georgian President, Eduard Shevardnadze, paid a three-day official visit to Greece in September 1997. According to Greece's President Konstandinos Stefanopoulos, his meeting with his Georgian counterpart was an opportunity 'for the greater expansion of ties in the economic and cultural fields' and to confirm the 'traditionally close ties of friendship and cooperation between Greece and Georgia'. Shevardnadze replied that the visit afforded him the chance to 'establish new principles for effective cooperation in the future'.[1] The visit became a landmark development demonstrating Greece`s increasing interest to the Caucasus region.

At first glance, Greece seems to have a series of reasons to move into the Caucasus. These reasons are mainly related to economics, politics and securty. The three countries of the Caucasus region have been regarded by the international community as important since their declarations of independence, and Athens has attempted to ensure that its interests are represented in the region. While Greek interests have included building new economic links with the republics, Athens's primary aim has been to develop allies against its main international rival, Turkey. To a large degree, Greek efforts to achieve this goal have created a security dilemma and inhibited the chances for peace and stability in this volatile region. Although Greece's ability to be an influential actor in the Caucasus is limited by geography and other factors, the nature of Greek policy in the region is nonetheless worthy of examination.

This chapter aims to discuss the relations between Greece and the three republics of the Caucasus within the context of regional security. It will explore Greek strategy in the Caucasus region and propose alternative policies to avoid the centuries-old illness of the security dilemma, which will be defined in terms of the fact that most of the ways in which a country seeks to increase its security have the unintended or intended effect of decreasing the security of others. According to Thucydides: 'What made war inevitable was the growth of Athenian power and fear which this caused in Sparta.'[2]

RELATIONS WITH ARMENIA

Greek Foreign Ministry officials paid a visit to Armenia on 29 September 1994 and noted, in a press conference, the special warmth in the relations between the two countries and the broad prospects for the development of mutually profitable cooperation in various areas. He emphasized his government's willingness to help Armenia both in the context of the European Union and its own resources. The Greek delegation included representatives of Greek industrial, entrepreneurial, trade and export circles, and the delegation established contacts with corresponding organizations in Armenia. A series of agreements were signed, ranging from the protection of investment to scientific–technical cooperation, and some others are being readied for signing.[3] These were the documents commonly seen on the diplomatic tables of all the newly independent states during their early years of independence, and aimed to create a necessary legal base for relations both at the governmental and private sector levels. The only visible development for the Armenian side was the food aid, medicine and medical equipment that the Greek delegation brought together.[4]

Both sides, however, did not hesitate to make 'grand claims' as usually seen in these kinds of diplomatic missions. Greece pointed out its desire to take part in the peace mission to the Nagorno-Karabakh conflict. The Deputy Foreign Minister of Armenia, Zuloyan, stated that both Armenia and Karabakh reject the possibility that Turkey would become involved in peacekeeping forces.[5] These statements meant in actuality nothing and only produced material for the hardliners of the interested countries and some terrorist organizations. As an obvious example, one Russian diplomat noted that: 'Armenia and Turkey would hardly be able to have trade and economic relations, much less political relations, that are purely bilateral ... There are not only historical but also strategic reasons for this, for Yerevan's main objective is to develop relations with Russia, Greece, Bulgaria and to a smaller extent with Syria and Iran.'[6] A member of the illegal Kurdistan Workers' Party (PKK) warned Greece and Armenia – with some logic – that 'if Turkey did not have the Kurds as an obstacle, Turkey would be in Armenia at this moment ... Turkey would no doubt have opened a front against Greece.'[7]

In April 1995, the Greek Cyprus Foreign Ministry put forward a proposal for Greek Cypriot troops to participate in the 3,000-strong peacekeeping force being established by the Organization of Security and Cooperation in Europe (OSCE). As the head of ministry's European Affairs Department stated, this attempt aims to 'develop the political prestige of Cyprus'.[8] As can be guessed, further development achieved nothing other than escalating regional tensions. In terms of 'grand projects', another macro scheme surfaced during the contacts of Greece's Chief of National Defense General Staff in Yerevan in July 1995. Armenian Foreign Minister Papazyan stressed the importance of Greece's support in the process of integrating Armenia into the European military and economic structures.[9]

Not much later, the focus in bilateral relations shifted to fields of security and military from issues related to technological cooperation, trade and development. This was an inevitable development, since bilateral trade relations and investments require substantial concrete steps and it is not possible to pursue such relations with vague agreements and promises.

Military cooperation between Greece and Armenia was on the top of the agenda during Armenia's President Levon Ter-Petrosyan's visit to Athens in the same month. Armenia's Major-General Arutyunyan said that military cooperation aims to strengthen the defense capability of the two countries.[10] It is not clear whether Armenia intended to be drawn this policy line, but Greek Defense Minister Arsenis gives hints that some circles in Greece aim to pull Yerevan into Athens's regional maneuvers. In a recent speech, Arsenis underlined the need for military cooperation with Russia, Armenia, Bulgaria, Iraq, Syria and Iran against Turkey.[11]

A flurry of high-level visits followed one another. The next meeting was between Greek Prime Minister Simitis and Armenian President Ter-Petrosyan in June 1996. Ter-Petrosyan also met his Greek counterpart, Stefanopoulos, and invited him to visit Armenia. Stefanopoulos expressed his feelings as follows: 'Bilateral relations are excellent and there are absolutely no problems shadowing them. Everyone is well aware of the Greek people's feelings toward the Armenian people. We have a history of friendly relations that goes back 2,000 years. During all periods of our history we were very close to each other. Now, we want to develop our excellent relations futher.'[12] If one sets aside the actual yield of relations between the two countries, the Greek President's words seem sincere and include very basic principles of mutual trust and peaceful relations. A prerequisite of such good neighborly relations is to assure other countries that any step taken will also increase regional well-being and does not constitute a threat to the other countries of the region. During this visit, the President of the Greek Chamber of Deputies, Kaklamanis, handed the Armenian President a copy of the Chamber's resolution adopted in spring 1996 on the recognition of the 1915 Armenian genocide.[13]

If one adds this to other policy statements discussed so far, these all lead to the conclusion that Greek decision makers had something very different in mind when they sat at the table with their Armenian counterparts. In this respect, military cooperation does not seem aimed at improving regional peace and stability. Indeed, such ties with Greece hamper the prospects of a Turkish–Armenian rapprochement and offer little direct benefit to Armenian security. Acknowledging this, the Turkish Defense Minister, Sungurlu, pointed out that he 'do[es] not know why Greece is seeking such relations in the Caucasus … Armenia, on the other hand, needs us because it depends on us for permission to use our airspace.'[14] From the Greeks' perspective, however, the motive behind the expansion of ties with Armenia is clear: Athens is seeking allies and influence to challenge Turkish interests in the Caucasus. Armenia, on the other hand, appears to view relations with Greece as a way to offset the increasing closeness between Turkey and Azerbaijan; Yerevan's efforts to break out of its growing international isolation as a result of the Nagorno-Karabakh conflict are also evident in its maintenance of close ties with Russia and Iran and in its recent overtures to Bulgaria and Syria.[15] In this regard, a Greek Foreign Ministry spokesman, answering a question on Turkey's reaction to the Greek–Armenian defense agreement, said that Greece wanted peaceful relations with all regional countries and that these relations were based on international law to promote bilateral and multifaceted cooperation.[16] Seemingly, Greece will continue a policy of peace and cooperation with all regional countries except Turkey.

These developments are also at odds with the attempts of the Yerevan leadership to normalize its relations with Turkey. Ter-Petrosyan recently argued that 'the sooner Turkey takes its place in the European Union, the better it will be for Armenia' underlining that it is Greece that is resisting Turkey's admittance to European structures.[17] There is a strong tendency among Turkish business circles to promote trade with Armenia.[18] This secret and unofficial diplomacy will largely depend on the Armenian government's willingness to cease regional tensions and to put an end to the speculations on Armenian help to the PKK.[19] An Armenian political observer, Grigoryan, pointed out that 'all these facts prompt the thought that the conclusion of the Greco-Armenian military alliance was by no means the independent fruit of Armenian foreign policy but was dictated to a large extent by Russian influence'.[20] Armenia, in this respect, wavers between its own interests and the security concerns of Greece and Russia.

In April 1997, Pangalos met with Armenia's President Levon Ter-Petrosian, Prime Minister Robert Kocharian and Parliament President B. Araktsian, as well as with the Patriarch of Armenia, Karekin I. This time Pangalos underlined the ongoing contacts with Iran and the representatives of the two countries agreed to develop relations in the framework of the tripartite cooperation between Greece, Iran and Armenia. He said that, 'Turkey's threats against Greece are unethical and illegal since they are contrary to international law, agreements and international practice.' Pangalos added that it should be realized once and for all in Ankara that the Ottoman Empire is dead, and there is no way to revive it.[21] The Greek Foreign Minister's main aim is to besiege Turkey rather than to develop relations with Armenia.

As can be observed, relations are almost restricted to military cooperation. Armenia's Prime Minister Kocharyan, and the Chief of Staff of the Greek National Defense Headquarters, Dzoganis, met in Yerevan in June and jointly declared that Armenia and Greece would exchange military intelligence and expand their joint training programs.[22] This declaration again increased regional tension and the Turkish Foreign Ministry spokesman, Atacanli, said that Turkey was closely watching the Greek–Armenian agreement, and added that the 'issue concerns the security of Turkey and for this reason it is showing the necessary sensitivity'.[23] The only visible interest on the Greek side was put forward by the National Defense Minister. He argued that one main Greek interest is to secure stability and peace in the Caucasus in order to make possible the construction of an oil pipeline between Burgas, Bulgaria and Alexandroupolis, Greece.[24] The Burgas–Alexandroupolis pipeline was conceptualized by Russia in 1995 in an effort to counter Turkey's move – for ostensibly environmental reasons – to restrict the amount of oil-tanker traffic through the Bosphorous Strait. Once completed, the pipeline would allow shipments of Caspian Sea oil exported via Russia's Black Sea port of Novorossisk to bypass the Bosphorous.[25] From the Armenian perspective, however, the Burgas–Alexandroupolis pipeline has little significance, and, indeed, the project may harm the prospect – however remote – for a future Caspian pipeline crossing Armenian territory.

Greek Defense Minister, Tsokhatzopoulos, shed significant light on Greece's security policy in the region, claiming said that Turkey is disputing and casting doubt on the status quo in this region. In his view, 'the response to these destabilizing factors lies in the following: first, international organizations should mobilize all their efforts to condemn all such attempts, and, second, the armed forces should be strengthened, as only a powerful defense can guarantee security in the region'.[26] Athens aims to create a regional security regime, which is based on different levels of cooperation with countries in the Caucasus and in the Middle East. Athens has a clear intention of reducing security of its imagined enemy, Turkey, and any possible coalition that Turkey may take part in. Greece's policy toward other two countries of Caucasus – Azerbaijan and Georgia – is the subject of the following section.

RELATIONS WITH GEORGIA AND AZERBAIJAN

Greece's approach to Azerbaijan in 1991 was strictly due to its own security concerns. Greece had worried that Azerbaijan would recognize Northern Cyprus. Azerbaijan's President Muttalibov, however, said that Azerbaijan would follow the position of the international community on the problem.[27]

Not much later, the Azerbaijani President and Greek Foreign Minister, Karolos Papoulias, met during the Black Sea Economic Cooperation Zone (BSEC) conference held in 1993. Two issues were on the agenda: cooperation with Greece, and entering into contact with the European Union. 'Our states,' Aliyev said, 'have good prospects for the development of bilateral relations'.[28] Aliyev tried to bring the Armenian–Azerbaijani conflict to the consideration of Papoullas but received the usual diplomatic response: Papoullas argued that Greece 'has always been a supporter of disputed questions being solved at the negotiating table, not with violence. We can not be indifferent to the problems of refugees and offer our services for a halt to an escalation of the conflict. Greece as a sovereign state and as the country that heads the European Union is ready to cooperate with Azerbaijan'.[29]

Athens's close relations with Armenia led to discontent in Azerbaijan. The Azeri newspaper *Zerkalo* argued that the developing relations between Turkey and Azerbaijan nudged Athens into open support for Armenia against Azerbaijan. It further added that close relations 'between Turkey and Azerbaijan prompted Athens to conclude a similar document with Armenia'.[30]

During an official visit to Baku in April 1997, Greece's Foreign Minister Pangalos told Aliyev that Greece is interested in Azerbaijani oil and is also eager to take an active part in projects to transport Baku's oil to Europe.[31] Aliyev responded to the question of whether Baku favored a Bulgarian–Greece pipeline that would bypass Turkey by saying: 'The route has not been decided. This is all speculation and do not believe everything you hear.'[32] In addition, Pangalos and his counterpart, Hasanov, signed three agreements on consular and cultural cooperation protocol between the two ministries.

The next high-level meeting was held again in Baku between the Greek Defense Minister, Tsokhatzopoulos, and Aliyev in July 1997. The Greek minister said that, being situated in the same geopolitical zone with the Caucasian region, Greece is vitally interested in peace and stability there. He added that 'nobody will stop us from implementing this'.[33] The Azerbaijani President replied, 'I understand that you have close relations with Armenia, but this should not hinder our cooperation,' and he also expressed perplexity over the planned joint Greek–Armenian military exercises: 'I thought about this and wondered why you are doing it.'[34]

The level of Greek–Georgian relations seems better than Greece's relations with Azerbaijan. The Georgian President expressed his feelings during a visit to Athens as follows: 'We have already achieved practical results in the economic and cultural spheres, as well as tourism. Greece will be taking an active role in implementing a project of universal significance, I mean the TRACECA [Europe–Caucasus–Asia transport corridor] project. Up to now, Greece has not been actively involved in the project, but I have had the feeling that the country has immense potential and that it should be involved in the project.'[35] Relations began to warm after November 1994 visit of the

Georgian Foreign Minister, Chikvaidze, to Greece. During this visit, five documents were signed, ranging from cooperation between the ministries of foreign affairs to agreements in the sphere of postal communication and telecommunications.[36] In the same month a Greek delegation was in Tbilisi to conduct an official visit.[37] As if to underline the strategic implications of developing relations, the Greek Deputy Minister of Economy was in Tbilisi to discuss agricultural and industrial cooperation between Greece and Georgia, and an agreement on economic and technological cooperation was signed.[38]

In May 1997 the Greek communications organization, OTE, and the building company, Hellax, signed a $14 million contract with Tblisi to build and operate fiber-optic networks in Georgia.[39] Such steps between the two countries seem more fruitful and address more the needs of Tbilisi. In September 1997 Shevardnadze paid a three-day visit to Athens. He was accompanied by a ministerial delegation and businessmen, as well as representatives of the 80,000 strong ethnic Greek community in Georgia, which he called the 'flesh and blood of the country'.[40] The sides discussed security and stability in the region, and stressed Georgia's considerable role in the Caucasus. The Georgian President thanked the Greek government for its support of Georgian territorial integrity, adding that 'the existence of stability in the Caucasus region is of great interest' to Greece and that 'this desire totally agrees with our desire.'[41]

Athens aims to provide a regional stability under a four-way partnership formula: Greece–Armenia–Georgia–Iran. The Armenian side supported this proposal and in January of 1997 a meeting of the ministers of foreign affairs of these countries was planned in Athens. However, it did not take place 'for technical reasons' and was postponed indefinitely. The reason most likely had to do with the position of Georgia, which appears more interested in a different four-way formula: Tbilisi–Baku–Ankara–Kiev.[42] Although Tblisi is certainly eager to broaden the quantity and quality of its foreign relationships, a goal of Georgian diplomacy since 1995 has been to promote the creation of a transport corridor linking Georgia, Azerbaijan and Central Asia to Europe via Turkey and Ukraine.[43] It should also be kept in mind that Turkey is Georgia's number-one trading partner, and Tblisi is unlikely to endanger either this relationship or the prospects for a Eurasian transport corridor for the sake of improving relations with Greece.[44]

CONCLUDING OBSERVATIONS: THE WIDER GEOPOLITICAL
PICTURE

Greek decision makers ignore the fact that reducing an imagined adversary's security – in this case Turkey – can reduce the state's own security. This security challenge shifts the focus of the adversary to employ counterpolicies, thereby making it harder to deter. In the Caucasian context, Greek activities encourage the three states – Azerbaijan, Armenia and Georgia – to join competing alliances and thus add to tensions in this volatile region. Athens also in effect restrains these new states' ability to follow independent policy lines. The main focus of attention is shifting to security concerns such as secure borders, strategic depth and control of resources that are valuable for building military capabilities.

Theoretically, although states exist in a condition of international anarchy that does not vary, there can be significant variation in the attractiveness of cooperative or competitive means. Political will is a precondition to trigger the search for means of cooperation and stability. As Glaser argues: 'Whether states can rely on unit-level information about others' motives can have equally important implications, enabling a state to be secure when it would otherwise be insecure, which in some cases supports more cooperative policies and in other cases more competitive ones.'[45] It seems more rational to seek cooperation in already existing schemes. In this case, the best way to foster regional peace and stability is to reconsider the Black Sea Economic Zone in a constructive way. Athens should pay attention to its potential role in this scheme as a European Union member.

The security-seeker position in Caucasia has led Athens feel more secure by attempting to increase its adversary's sentiment of encirclement. The adversary then employs additional means in order to restore its security capability. Turkey's increasing cooperation with Georgia and Azerbaijan and Greece's attempts to widen its regional influence should be re-evaluated in this regard. As outlined above, a series of geopolitical relationships are emerging in Eurasia. On one side are Russia and Iran along with a series of smaller powers, including Greece and Armenia. On the other side are Turkey, Azerbaijan, Georgia, Ukraine and, as recent developments indicate, Israel.[46] Also on the rise in the region is the influence and engagement of the United States and the European Union, both of which seek to tap into the vast energy reserves of the Caspian region. The emerging security environment is thus one in which two blocs of states are in increasing competition with one another. Therefore, policies that promote the further emergence of a bipolar order will have the potential to aggravate regional tensions and introduce new security concerns in this important yet unstable region.

In geopolitical environments in which competition rather than cooperation is the rule of the day, countries are quick to impute malevolent intentions upon their perceived adversaries, even if the adversaries' activities are ambiguous in nature. Moreover, under such conditions, all players are likely to view events in a zero-sum fashion in which a gain by one side is perceived as a loss by the other. Unfortunately, the Caucasus is emerging as such an environment. Intentionally or not, Greek activities have aimed to increase Athens's influence and prestige in the region vis-à-vis Turkey, but in actuality Greece has contributed little to either the prosperity or the security of the Caucasian states. If the solidification of a two-bloc security order in the region is to be prevented, surrounding states must learn to put aside their historical animosities and move together toward a new era of peace, stability and cooperation.

NOTES

1. Athens News Agency, Athens, in English, 15 September 1997 in BBC Summary of World Broadcast, SU/03027, 18 September 1997, F.
2. Robert Jervis, 'Realism, Game Theory and Cooperation', *World Politics* 40, No. 3, (1988) p. 318
3. *Respublika Armeniya*, Yerevan, in Russian, 30 September 1994, p. 1, in FBIS-USR, 30 September 1994, p. 104.
4. *Snark*, Yerevan, in English, 22 November 1994, in FBIS-SOV, 9 November 1995, p. 226.
5. Ibid.
6. Interfax, Moscow, in English, 20 December 1994, in FBIS-SOV, 11 August 1995, p. 245
7. *Kiriakatiki Elevtherotipia*, Athens, in Greek, 12 February 1995, p. 23 in FBIS-WEU, 18 November 1995, p. 52.
8. *Cyprus Mail*, Nicosia, in English, 14 April 1995, p. 7, in FBIS-WEU, 14 November 1995, p. 73.
9. *Elevtherotipia*, Athens, in Greek, 22 July 1995, p. 4, in FBIS-SOV, 7 November 1995, p. 141.
10. ITAR-TASS, Moscow, in English, 23 July 1995, in FBIS-SOV, 7 November 1995, p. 141.
11. *Kathimerini*, Athens, in Greek, 2 April 1996, p. 2, in FBIS-WEU, 4 April 1996, p. 65.
12. *Elliniki Radhiofonia*, Athens, in Greek, 17 June 1996, in FBIS-WEU, 19 June 1996, p. 118.
13. Armenia's Radio First, in Armenian, 18 June 1996, in FBIS-SOV, 18 June 1996, p. 119.
14. Anatolia, Ankara, in Turkish, 18 June 1996, in FBIS WEU, 21 June 1996, p. 120.
15. Michael P. Croissant, 'U.S. Interests in the Caspian Sea Basin', *Comparative Strategy* 16, No. 4 (October–December 1997) p. 360.
16. *Elliniki Radhiofonia*, Athens, in Greek, 20 June 1996, in FBIS-WEU, 21 June 1996, p. 120.
17. *Zerkalo*, Baku, in Russian, no.31, 3 August 1996, p. 14, in FBIS-SOV, 29 October 1996, p. 208-S.
18. Fatih Cekirge, 'Ermenistan'la Yeni Donem', (New Era in Relations with Armenia), *Sabah*, 24 August 1997, p. 4
19. The Secretary General of the Turkish Armed forces, Erol Ozkasnak, made a statement at a news conference, in June 1997, that Armenia had supplied antiaircraft missiles to Kurds via Turkish territory with which two Turkish military helicopters were shot down, in the same month, in Iraq's airspace. See 'Foreign Ministry Denies Charges of Arms Sales to Kurds', *Asbarez*, 8 June 1997, online.
20. *Zerkalo*, Baku, in Russian, No. 31, 3 August 1996, p. 14, in FBIS-SOV, 29 October 1996, p. 208-S.
21. *Sabah*, 27 April 1997, p. 6.
22. Interfax, Moscow, in English, 20 June 1997, in FBIS-SOV, 23 June 1997, p. 171.
23. Athens News Agency, Athens, in English, 24 June 1997, in FBIS-WEU, 25 June 1997, p. 175.
24. *Elliniki Radhiofonia*, Athens, in Greek, 27 June 1997, in FBIS-WEU, 30 June 1997, p. 178.
25. Jennifer DeLay, 'Bulgaria-Greece Pipeline to be Built on Business Grounds', *Pipeline News*, No. 34, pp. 19–25 October 1996, online.
26. *Noyan Tapan*, Yerevan, in Russian, 17 July 1997, in FBIS-SOV, 18 July 1997, p. 198.
27. 'Azerbaijan will not Recognize Northern Cyprus', *Russian Press Digest*, 21 November 1991, available in LEXIS/NEXIS, World Library, Allwld File.
28. Bakinskiy Rabochiy, Baku, in Russian, 21 June 1994, pp. 1–2, in FBIS-SOV, 14 November 1995, p. 122.
29. Ibid.
30. *Zerkalo*, Baku, in Russian, No. 25, 22 June 1996, p. 23 in FBIS-SOV, 18 July 1997, p. 138-S; for a similar view see, 'Instability No Stranger to the Transcaucasus', *Jamestown Fortnight in Review* 1, No. 1, 28 June 1996, online.

31. Athens News Agency, Athens, in English, 12 April 1997, in FBIS-WEU, 15 April 1997, p. 102.
32. *Turkish Daily News*, 2 November 1994, p. A3.
33. Athens News Agency, Athens, in English, 21 July 1997, in FBIS-WEU, 22 July 1997, p. 202.
34. *Turan*, Baku, in Russian, in 18 July 1997, in FBIS-SOV, 22 July 1997, p. 200.
35. Radio Tblisi, Tblisi, in Georgian, 22 September 1997, in FBIS-SOV, 23 September 1997, p. 265.
36. *Rezonansi*, Tblisi, in Georgian, 15–16 November 1994, p. 2, in FBIS-SOV, 9 November 1995, p. 226.
37. Contact Information Agency, Tblisi, in Russian, 24 November 1994, in FBIS-SOV, 9 November 1995, p. 227.
38. Radio Tblisi, Tblisi, in Georgian, 13 January 1995, in FBIS-SOV, 19 November 1995, p. 9.
39. ITAR-TASS, Moscow, in English, 19 May 1997, in FBIS-WEU, 22 May 1997, p. 139.
40. Athens News Agency, Athens, in English, 15 September 1997, in FBIS-WEU, 17 September 1997, p. 158.
41. Athens News Agency, Athens, in English, 16 September 1997, in FBIS-WEU, 17 September 1997, p. 259.
42. *Moskovskiye Novosti*, Moscow, in Russian, No. 29, 20–7 July 1997, in FBIS-UMA, 23 July 1997, p. 203.
43. Liz Fuller, 'New Geo-Political Alliances on Russia's Southern Rim,' RFE/RL Newsline 1, No. 2, part 1, 16 November 1997, via the Internet, http://www.rferl.org; Jennifer DeLay, 'Georgia Will Act as Conduit for Azeri Crude Oil, Liquified Gas Going to Ukraine', *Pipeline News*, No. 36, 2–8 November 1996, online.
44. Roland Eggleston, 'The East: Black Sea States Expect Economic Boom', *RFE/RL Daily Report*, 30 June 1997, via the Internet, http://www.rferl.org.
45. Charles L. Glaser, 'The Security Dilemma Revisited', *World Politics* 50, No. 1 (1997), p. 174.
46. Greece's Foreign Minister Pangalos recently said that if the Turkish–Israeli relations 'evolves into a defense alliance with political as well as military cooperation, it would be disturbing for Greece and for Arab nations'. Agence France Press, 21 December 1997, available in LEXIS/NEXIS, World Library, Allwld File; for more information on the emerging role of Israel in this region see Bulent Aras, 'Post-Cold-War Realities: Israel's Strategy in Azerbaijan and Central Asia', *Middle East Policy* 5, No. 4 (January 1998) pp. 68–81.

IRANIAN POLICY TOWARD THE CASPIAN SEA REGION BASIN

Numerous and significant changes have occurred in the world during the past ten years. The rise of the young democracies in Eastern Europe and the founding of independent states in Central Asia and Transcaucasia are among the visible and undoubtedly positive international results. These changes have also created conditions in which the need for cooperation and mutual understanding among countries is felt more acutely than ever.

The Islamic Republic of Iran is in a particularly favorable situation as regards the newly independent states of Central Asia and Transcaucasia. Iran has acquired new neighbors to the north with which it shares a desire to develop cooperation on a bilateral as well as a multilateral regional basis. The sense of historical community between newly independent countries to the north and Iran creates opportunities for the development of cooperation on and coordination of many activities in the region.[1]

In March 1992, Iran proposed creating a bloc of Caspian countries within a free-trade zone or integrated association. On the basis of that proposal, the Organization of Cooperation of the Caspian Countries (OCCC) was formed that same year. OCCC includes Azerbaijan, Iran, Kazakhstan, Russia and Turkmenistan and has its headquarters in Tehran. The organization is intended to deal mainly with problems of fishing, navigation, environmental protection and oil and gas exploration and production in the Caspian Sea and on its shores.

Iran's leaders have also looked beyond the Caspian region and have proposed the creation of an international organization of gas-producing and exporting countries, a kind of 'gas OPEC' (Organization of Petroleum Exporting Countries) but without the participation of North Atlantic Treaty Organization countries. It was to include Azerbaijan, Iran, Russia, Turkmenistan and Uzbekistan. The idea was endorsed by Algeria, Venezuela, Indonesia, Iraq, Libya, and Nigeria – countries that, along with Iran and Russia, are the main producers and exporters of natural gas. There is no doubt that Iran's policy is not only aimed at forestalling the region's Westernization or Turkification but is intended to expand its own regional influence. Iran has borders with Azerbaijan, Turkmenistan and Kazakhstan to the north and eleven other countries to the east, west and south, including oil-rich Arab states. Iranian analysts point out that, by taking advantage of this proposal, their country can serve as a bridge between the Caspian Sea and the Persian Gulf, the two major energy-producing regions in the world.[2]

This chapter will discuss Iranian interests in the Caspian Sea basin from a wide geopolitical perspective. A discussion on the Caspian Sea legal debate will be followed by a look at Tehran's relations with littoral states and the policies of the United States and Turkey vis-à-vis Iran. This study argues that Iran is the key to peace and stability in the newly emerging northern tier of the Middle East and that the current Iranian potential should be cultivated through all possible means.

DEBATE OVER THE CASPIAN: SEA OR LAKE?

For the past three years, the five littoral states of the Caspian – Azerbaijan, Russia, Kazakhstan, Turkmenistan and Iran – have been involved in a dispute over whether this body of water should legally be designated as a *lake* or a *sea*. This arcane debate stems from the dramatically divergent methods of dividing the Caspian's resources that would follow from the choice of term. The Caspian contains some of the largest deposits of oil and natural gas in the world, and so billions of dollars ride on the outcome.[3]

Under the 1982 United Nations Convention on the Law of the Sea,[4] if a body of water is a sea, those countries that border it have the right to claim as their own the waters closest to their shores,[5] with exclusive rights of resource exploitation within those waters. Technically, coastal states are entitled to claim as their sovereign territory only those waters within twelve miles of their shores, but they are allowed to exploit as their 'exclusive economic zone' those waters within two hundred miles of the edge of their territorial waters.[6] Therefore, under the *sea* designation, those states in closest geographical proximity to the largest oil deposits will reap the greatest economic rewards from the exploitation of the water body; hydrocarbon deposits. Unfortunately, however, the UN Convention never defines the term *sea,* and so this agreement is of no help in determining the Caspian; legal status.

If a body of water is not a sea and thus not regulated by the UN Convention, then by default it falls under the classification of a *lake*. While no international convention defines this term or establishes a rule for dividing such a body's resources, precedent has established that those countries bordering on a lake are to divide its resources equally among them, as has been done with the Great Lakes on the US–Canada border and with Lake Chad in Africa.[7]

38

The positions taken by each of the five littoral states of the Caspian over the body's legal status are predictable when one considers the geographical distribution of deposits beneath its waters. Azerbaijan and Kazakhstan both assert firmly that the Caspian is an inland sea, and it is these states that have the richest deposits within what would be their exclusive economic zones under the UN Convention.[8] Azerbaijan is the more vocal of the two and has even written into the text of its constitution the assertion that the waters off its shore are within its exclusive sovereignty.[9]

Russia, whose waters have perhaps the most meager deposits, has been the most outspoken in advocacy of the *lake* characterization. The Russian government has sent to the UN General Assembly a document titled 'The Position of the Russian Federation with Regard to the Status of the Caspian Sea', in which it asserts that the UN Convention is not applicable in this case. Russia pointed out that the legal status of this water body was defined previously by treaties negotiated between the Soviet Union and Iran in 1921 and 1940, which cast the Caspian as a saltwater lake whose resources were to be divided communally.[10] Russia has, however, more recently evinced some willingness to compromise. At a regional conference in November 1996, its Foreign Minister, Yevgeny Primakov, came forward with a settlement offer that would have allowed each littoral state exclusive economic rights within 72 kilometers (45 miles) of its shore as well as in those hydrocarbon fields beyond this limit where extraction had already begun.[11] This proposal was not con-sidered seriously by Azerbaijan, as 45 miles of exclusive ownership is a far cry from the roughly 212 miles contemplated by the UN Convention. More recently, Russia took a different stance. On 28 April 1998, the Russian and Kazakh presidents announced in Moscow their agreement to a pact for the division of the resources underneath the Caspian seabed. According to this agreement, signed on 6 July 1998, the Caspian seabed will be shared by all the littoral states.[12]

Iran also adjoins an area of the Caspian with relatively meager mineral deposits, and not surprisingly its position traditionally has been very close to that of Russia. Tehran supported the previous Russian suggestion that the UN Convention has no application, adding that all issues related to the Caspian's exploitation should be settled by the five states that touch its shores, without any external interference.[13] The 1998 Russian policy shift, however, was not well regarded by Tehran. A spokesman for Iran's Foreign Ministry, referring to the agreement between Russia and Kazakhstan, emphasized that 'any bilateral agreement which is incompatible with the existing legal regime of the Caspian Sea is not valid and not recognized officially by the Islamic Republic of Iran'.[14]

Turkmenistan has been inconsistent on this issue. Initially it supported the characterization of the Caspian as a sea, but at the end of 1996 it began to move toward the Russian–Iranian camp. Early in 1998, however,

Turkmenistan returned to its original position when President Saparmurad Niyazov came forward with the assertion that two oilfields previously claimed by Azerbaijan, both among the richest deposits in the Caspian, lie in the Turkmen sector.[15]

The countries involved in this dispute are all convinced that the anticipated revenue from the exploitation of the Caspian's mineral reserves will provide a significant boost to their economies and bring in much-needed foreign currency. The recent shift in Russia's position brought Turkmenistan and Iran closer on the matter of sea versus lake.

IRAN'S RELATIONS WITH AZERBAIJAN AND KAZAKHSTAN

Iran's interaction with post-independence Azerbaijan may be characterized as a love-hate relationship. A 1995 US statement about Iran's participation in the Azerbaijan International Oil Company (AIOC) represented a turning point in Iranian–Azeri relations with regard to the Caspian region. Previously, Tehran had followed a policy of political cooperation and searched for every possible means to increase its involvement in the Caspian basin. The statement of the US Embassy in Baku, in which it voiced opposition to Iran's participation in an agreement signed by Azerbaijan and a consortium of Western oil companies, directly struck at Iranian policy toward the Caspian. Tehran remained in an ambiguous posture for a brief period thereafter. Soon it formulated a new policy, oriented toward much closer relations with Russia and increasing political and economic relations with Armenia while adopting a cautious policy toward Azerbaijan.

The 1993 removal of President Abulfaz Elchibey from office in Azerbaijan had excited decision makers in Tehran and created opportunities for developing relations with Azerbaijan. Elchibey's removal was regarded in Iran as an end to Azerbaijan's highly pro-Turkish and pro-Western policy of the previous years. Azerbaijan's positions had concerned Iranian leaders on a number of issues. As about 20 million people in northern Iran have their origins in Azerbaijan, statements of Azeri officials about a possible Greater Azerbaijan uniting the two sides of the Aras River had raised obvious concern. Malik Mufti's argument that 'Turkish nationalism in Azerbaijan threatens Iran's very existence'[16] may seem exaggerated, but it serves as a barometer of some feeling in Tehran. As Gussein Baguirov, rector of Baku West University, noted: 'Tehran is not honest in its relations with Baku and regards it as a big headache.'[17] Azerbaijan's new president, Heydar Aliyev, paid a visit to Tehran in June 1994. The agenda for his talks included the delivery of diesel fuel from Azerbaijan to Iran and the transportation of Iranian gas to Azerbaijan's Nakhichevan Autonomous Republic. An agreement on the delivery of 1.6 million tons of diesel fuel had been signed in late 1993. The president of the State Oil Company of Azerbaijan, Natik Aliyev, called it a 'document in force' and said that Azerbaijan delivered to Iran 500,000 tons of oil in 1994. The expectation of greater cooperation in political and economic realms prevented both sides from bringing the issues concerning the status of the Caspian Sea and prospective pipelines into the discussion.[18]

In this honeymoon era, Azerbaijan also tried to expand cooperation to the political realm and succeeded in crafting an agreement, signed by both presidents, sharply blaming Armenia for aggression. According to Azerbaijan's Foreign Minister, Hasan Hasanov, this was the first time that Armenian aggression against Azerbaijan was assessed in a joint Azeri–Iranian political document.[19] Although the Azeri government agreed in general terms in 1994 that Iran would make use of Azerbaijan's possibilities in the Caspian Sea, and Azerbaijan would make use of Iran's, the concrete forms of such cooperation in oil, fishing and shipping were not defined.[20] This cautious approach was an early signal of the intensifying conflicts of coming years.

In late January 1995, Iranian media commented on the aforementioned press release issued by the US Embassy in Baku. The statement clearly indicated that US oil companies would boycott the contract if the National Iranian Oil Company (NIOC) participated. The Iranian Embassy in Baku responded immediately, arguing that the statement testified to Washington's intent 'to establish control over the natural resources of other states and to interfere directly in their domestic affairs'.[21]

This was a surprising development, since the Azeri government had agreed in November 1994 to the transfer of a 5 per cent share of the contract to NIOC. The Iranian media also claimed that US companies were anxious to be assured of the participation of both Iran and Russia, which have extensive experience in oil production and export. Iranian media also argued that the statement issued by the US Embassy was an outrageous insult to the government of Azerbaijan and an infringement of the national sovereignty of that country.[22] United States policy, however, is very clear. Washington has said that it is against any involvement of Iran in Caspian oil deals or the transport of petroleum to be extracted. The State Department declared that 'our policy is to oppose projects which could provide Iran with political or financial benefits'.[23]

On the eve of this turmoil, an Azeri government delegation in February 1995 had traveled to Tehran to negotiate dates for the delivery from Iran of electricity and food to the Nakhichevan Autonomous Republic under an earlier agreement. In addition, a series of talks were held on construction of a natural gas pipeline to link Iran to Nakhichevan, a refinery to process oil received from Iran, and other long-term energy projects for the autonomous republic. The delegation was not authorized to discuss the possibility of Iran's membership in an international consortium formed to develop offshore Azerbaijani oilfields in the Caspian.[24] Azerbaijan, not to frustrate Iran any more, strongly denied rumors that 5 per cent of Iran's share had been given to Turkey. A senior Azeri diplomat stated: 'The share of the Republic of Azerbaijan is 20 percent, and on the basis of an official agreement, that country has given 5 percent of its shares to Iran and 5 percent to a Turkish oil company.'[25]

Azerbaijan again tried to repair relations with Iran when its presidential adviser, Vafa Gholizadeh, expressed regret on the rejection of Iran's request for participation in the agreement between the republic and a consortium of Western oil companies and Turkey.[26] Azeri officials repeatedly expressed Baku's readiness for cooperation with Tehran to explore other oilfields in Azerbaijan and disclaimed allegations that the United States had made Azerbaijan abstain from cooperation with Iran.

In December 1995, Iran rejected an Azeri proposal to participate in the development of the Shakh–Deniz gas-condensate field located in the Azeri Caspian sector.[27] The Iranian Deputy Foreign Minister, Mahmud Vaezi, said that the possibility had been raised by the President of Azerbaijan. Vaezi's response was cold and a landmark development in the new cautious Iranian approach toward Baku: 'We will study the received information and will give answer soon.'[28] Despite Tehran's hesitancy, pragmatism has prevailed, resulting in an agreement between SOCAR and Iran's Oil Industries Engineering and Construction Company (a subsidiary of NIOC) on the transfer of a stake of 10 per cent in a gas project in Azerbaijan.[29]

Kazakhstan has taken a more balanced attitude than Azerbaijan and has preferred to keep its door open to both Iran and the United States. President Nursultan Nazarbayev has said that, with regard to Iran, Kazakhstan 'takes into account the US's special attitude to Iran and its close cooperation with Chevron, but at the same time, it is the shortest way to the Persian Culf and we shall not reject it, because we lay more emphasis on economic interests, not political ones'.[30] Besides the United States and Iran, Moscow is an important factor in the foreign relations of Almaty. Kazakhstan's northern neighbor has an important leverage: the quota of the Kazakh oil shipment transferred through Russian territory. Moscow keeps this advantage alive in the diplomatic arena, arguing that 'we will increase shipments of your oil across our oil and gas pipelines, and you will alter your views on the borders dividing up the Caspian'.[31]

The setting up of an international oil consortium in Azerbaijan was welcomed by Kazakhstan, as such an arrangement will enable it to transport up to 10 million tons of Kazakh oil a year to Baku. Almaty also has alternatives to the Caspian Sea over which it can move its oil to market: through Iran to the Persian Gulf and through Afghanistan to the Pakistani port of Karachi.[32] Tehran seems aware of its geopolitical advantages and aims to transfer this advantage into cold cash by using its territory as a gateway for Kazakh oil.

Iran and Kazakhstan issued a joint statement in May 1996, at the end of the visit of President Nazarbayev to Iran, expressing their willingness to benefit further from joint ventures and public and private investments in the areas of gas and oil development, transportation, industry, trade, agriculture and mining. Terming as suitable the transfer of Kazakhstan's oil and gas to international markets via Iran, the two countries have begun studying ways and means for the implementation of both oil and gas pipeline projects from western Kazakhstan to northern Iran and eventually to the Persian Gulf.[33] The main issue at stake is the transporting of Kazakh oil to the Gulf; the sides agreed on an oil swap as a short-term solution. The Kazakh–Iranian agreement on oil exchanges, which took five years to negotiate, came into effect in early 1998. Under its terms, Kazakhstan will supply 2 million tons of oil a year through the Caspian port of Aktau to Iran's northern regions. Iran will put forward the same amount of oil through its terminals in the Persian Gulf for sale on the world market.

Kazakh Oil and Gas Ministry officials said that five tankers would deliver the oil. Each has already made one trip, delivering a total of 25,000 tons to Iran's Caspian ports. However, experts say that the five tankers can deliver no more than 100,000 tons a month instead of the planned 160,000 to 170,000.[34] This arrangement is believed to benefit the Iranians, as deliveries from the Caspian would replace oil piped from the south over hundreds of miles of desert to supply northern Iran. It also offers potential advantages to the oil companies and Azerbaijan's government as an economic means of getting oil to an ocean port and also an alternative route to the world marketplace in a volatile environment where pipelines could fall victim to politics and violence.[35]

IRAN AND RUSSIA/TURKMENISTAN

In October 1994, the Russian Federation submitted for consideration by all Caspian states a draft agreement on preservation and use of bioresources of the Caspian Sea. At about the same time, Iran proposed a treaty on regional cooperation in the Caspian Sea using the following rationale: 'The Russian efforts to accelerate the conclusion of the aforesaid important treaties that correspond to the interests of all the Caspian states, unfortunately, encounters [sic] inertia that cannot be described other than an attempt to avoid the establishment of a new international-legal regime for the Caspian Sea. At the same time, some Caspian nations are undertaking unilateral actions, ignoring principles and norms of the international law, and trying to achieve unilateral benefits to the prejudice of rights and interests of other Caspian nations.'[36]

Subsequently, the Iranian ambassador in Moscow told the Russian government that Tehran and Moscow have long-term common interests in the Caspian Sea and could uphold their cooperation within the framework of the projected organization of the Caspian Sea littoral states. Iranian officials said the Islamic Republic is ready to offer help in oil-related issues, including protection of the environment of the Caspian.[37]

Turkmenistan is quite in favor of the Iranian position on the status of the Caspian Sea and the participation of Iran in the extraction of oil and gas from this contested region. Iran's Deputy Foreign Minister, Vaezi, arrived in Ashkabad in February 1995, on the first leg of a trip to the capitals of the Central Asian states. He was welcomed by the Foreign Minister, Boris Shikhmurdov. During their talks, the two officials reviewed relations between Tehran and Ashkabad and agreed that closer bilateral relations would promote peace and security in the region. Iran repeated its traditional stance, referring to the Caspian Sea as 'the Sea of Cooperation' adding that the adoption of any decision relating to the Caspian should be based on the concurrence of all countries bordering the world's largest inland sea.'[38]

According to Mehmet Turna of Ashkabad Turkmenbashi University, Turkmenistan, which is now likely to be one of the most prosperous countries of the former Soviet Union, will build a pipeline through Iran despite the warnings of the Western powers.[39] In late summer 1994, Turkmenistan, Iran and Turkey signed an agreement to build a gas pipeline across Iran and Turkey to serve the countries of Europe. Turkmenistan's gas pipeline to Iran was planned for completion in March 1997. The Turkmenistan Foreign Minister was quoted by *Petroleum Argus* as saying at an Ashkabad conference that his country would start pumping gas to Iran on 1 September 1997 through the 140-kilometer pipeline. Mehdi Hosseini, head of exploration at NIOC, was also said to have revealed that half of the pipeline, which is being constructed despite US pressure to limit cooperation with Iran, was already completed. The pipeline is the first new gas export line from the Caspian to bypass Russia and is seen as holding tremendous implications for future sales of Iranian and Turkmen gas to Turkey and Europe.[40]

Despite these attempts, there is a long way to go to complete this project. The statements and willingness of officials in Tehran and Ashkabad has not succeeded in bringing Turkmen gas to Iran yet. In addition, so far only a few concrete steps have been taken to build a pipeline between Turkey and Iran. Work is being done at the same time on a grandiose plan to build a gas pipeline across Iran (or even Afghanistan) to Pakistan. Turkmenistan's government realizes that any chance to create a 'Kuwait of gas' depends on the goodwill of Iran's rulers, who have not concealed their intention of stepping up their influence in the Muslim areas of the former Soviet Union.[41]

A Russian senior diplomat, Albert Chernyshev, has noted that a Russian governmental commission has visited all five countries of the Caspian basin and achieved mutual understanding with Turkmenistan and Iran. Azerbaijan, however, insisted on its own position, while Kazakhstan's positions fall between those of Azerbaijan and Russia. Chernyshev said: 'We hope that it will be possible to settle these problems in a civilized way.'[42]

Russia's Foreign Minister Primakov, in a March 1996 joint press conference with his Iranian counterpart, Ah Akbar Velayati, called Iranian–Russian joint cooperation in settling regional disputes 'important' and said the two sides were in agreement on the necessity of extending the ceasefire among warring factions and continuing peace talks in Tajikistan. Velayati said Iran and Russia would draft long-term cooperation plans for the Caspian Sea given the suitable atmosphere of cooperation in the region, and he noted that the Russian President, Boris Yeltsin, had stressed the need for the expansion of full-scale relations with Tehran as a guarantee for regional peace and security.

Primakov welcomed Iran's proposal for setting up a cooperation council of Caspian Sea states and said Russian Foreign Ministry officials were studying the legal and economic basis of the idea. He added that, in line with the proposal, Russia would hold talks with the republics of Azerbaijan, Kazakhstan and Turkmenistan.[43]

Talks within the Commonwealth of Independent States have revealed common elements of approach to the status of the Caspian Sea. It was emphasized that a unique approach was necessary when determining the legal status of this unique body of water. Both Turkmenistan and Russia want a consensual approach by the Caspian littoral states when developing the biological resources of the Caspian Sea. It has been noted in this context that any unilateral decision might have undesirable consequences and that a mechanism is needed to carry out the necessary consultations and also to set up a standing body to resolve the problems relating to use of the sea. Seyyed Talibi, Iran's ambassador to Turkmenistan, supported this idea. In a March 1998 conversation with the deputy Russian Prime Minister, he confirmed his country's intention to participate in all consultations.[44] But, with the recent shifting in the Russian position, one may raise questions about the future of relations between Iran and Russia as they relate to the Caspian.

The visit to Tehran in January 1996 by Turkmenistan's President Niyazov was important in terms of developing relations with Iran. The joint press communiqué issued at the conclusion of the visit emphasized that valuable and important steps had been taken to increase and strengthen relations between the two countries and to cooperate in finding peaceful solutions to the existing crises in the region, including those of Tajikistan, Afghanistan and Karabakh. In this communiqué the two sides also expressed concern over the unilateral and uncontrolled exploitation of the Caspian Sea and stressed the need to establish a legal regime based on the joint exploitation of the sea by all the countries bordering it. Iran also called for a meeting of the foreign ministers of these countries and adoption of necessary decisions to protect the environment of this unique sea.[45]

In November 1996, the foreign ministers of Russia, Turkmenistan and Iran signed in Ashkabad a memorandum on cooperation among the three concerning oil and gas development in the Caspian Sea and invited Azerbaijan and

Kazakhstan to join. Russia's Primakov told the Tass news agency: 'We plan to create a joint company to develop and produce hydrocarbons in the offshore areas of the three states.'[46] A 1998 Moscow meeting of Russian, Iranian and Turkmenistan delegations, about which Kazakhstan was not informed, gave rise to rumors that a secret diplomatic game is being launched around issues pertaining to the Caspian.

President Mohammad Khatami of Iran, in a letter to Turkmenistan's President Niyazov, called on the sea's littoral states to draw up a legal regime for the world's largest inland sea. Khatami said: 'Peace and cooperation are possible through common sense and unanimity of views, and the Caspian states should work to determine the legal status of the sea so that its resources can be utilized lawfully.' An Iranian official in delivering the letter stressed that unilateral action by littoral states is contrary to the interests of neighboring states.[47]

Azerbaijan's Foreign Minister Hasanov said a new Russian–Iranian–Turkmen company 'will be unable to claim participation in developing the Azerbaijani section of the Caspian against Azerbaijan's will or without its initiative'.[48] Kazakhstan's Deputy Foreign Minister, Vyacheslav Gizzatov, added: 'The company will not operate where Azerbaijan and Kazakhstan operate.'[49] The prospects for Russian–Iranian–Turkmen cooperation, however, have been restricted since the recent Russian–Kazakh agreement on the legal status of the Caspian Sea.

Turkmenistan's President Niyazov, during his visit to Washington in April 1998, agreed to let the United States finance a feasibility study on construction of an oil and gas pipeline under the Caspian. He also signed deals with Mobil and Exxon and was fêted by American energy companies.[50] The US administration stressed the importance of the neutral status of Turkmenistan as a bulwark against Iranian influence.

THE ROLES OF THE US AND TURKEY

As has been discussed above, Tehran regards the United States as the main obstacle on its path to reaching oil ambitions in the Caspian region. The Conoco case shows clearly that the Iranian administration is eager to deal with US companies.

Two months after the January 1995 declaration by the United States Embassy in Baku, the US company Conoco and NIOC signed an agreement in Tehran.[51] The White House press secretary Michael McCurry described the $1 billion agreement as legal, but he also added that it is 'not a helpful development', since Washington seeks 'to bring pressure to bear on Iran to get them to behave in the world community'.[52] Washington then proceeded to bar US companies from signing deals to develop Iran's oilfields, thus blocking the arrangement between Tehran and Conoco. As an Iranian daily noted, Iran had made it clear that it will not compromise on this issue. It further argued that 'Iran has enough ways and means at its disposal to thwart US attempts at domination. It is not advisable for the Azeri Government to allow its foreign policy to come under US influence.'[53]

Azerbaijan's decision in April 1995 to cancel a deal allowing NIOC to take part in an international consortium further frustrated Iran. The daily *Iran News,* close to the government, accused the leaders of Azerbaijan of having 'pocketed US dollars' from the consortium's Western companies to push NIOC aside.[54] In addition to these events, Washington took a decisive stance against any pipeline project that would pass through Iranian territory. The region witnessed increasing US diplomatic activity in favor of a Baku–Ceyhan pipeline that would transfer Caspian oil through Turkey. US officials also sought to include Kazakh oil via an extension from Baku to the Kazakh shores of the Caspian.

An Iranian Deputy Foreign Minister, Abbas Maleki, deplored the US policy of penalizing international oil companies that made investment in the Iranian oil and gas industry. Speaking at the Fourth Conference on Middle East Petroleum and Gas, Maleki said Iran had already shown its desire to cooperate with all international companies that are ready to share technology and help Iran develop its resources. But, he said, 'We are facing a political challenge from some countries which are openly interfering in our internal affairs with no respect to the international law' and added that, as one eminent economist put it, 'where politics and economic objectives clash, it is the former not the latter which will ultimately fail'.[55]

Given that Turkey hopes to continue to play a significant role in the exploitation of Azerbaijan's oil reserves through participation in international consortia, and expects to become host to at least one of the pipelines that will carry oil to the West, Turkey's interests in the resolution of the dispute over the Caspian's legal status are closely aligned with those of Azerbaijan. Iran maintains its stance that all issues related to the Caspian's exploitation should be settled by the five states that touch its shores, without any external interference. For this reason, the Caspian policy of Iran is watched closely by Turkey. Azerbaijan's deteriorating relations with Iran – in the aftermath of the decision to exclude Tehran from the production deal – created an impetus in Baku for further development of relations with Ankara. Turkey has welcomed Baku's approach, since it has a major stake in carrying Azeri oil to world markets.

In the midst of all these events, an Iranian–Turkish–European natural gas pipeline project has been proposed. This project would take Iranian natural gas to Europe through Turkey. Talks on this subject are expected to continue. In the short term, Iran and Turkey have already signed an agreement that envisages the former selling 2 billion cubic meters of natural gas annually to the latter.[56]

47

Turkey plans to begin purchase of natural gas from Turkmenistan in 1998. Turkish officials have stated that, by signing an agreement with Iran as well, it could create a competitive environment that could lead to a decrease in the cost of natural gas in Turkey. In this regard, Russia is another alternative, and Botas, the Turkish state-run pipeline concern, may form a partnership or joint consortium with the Russian companies Gazprom and Gama. Botas would hold 35 per cent of the shares.[57]

Taking a further step, Turkey called a meeting in March 1998 of foreign ministers from Azerbaijan, Turkmenistan, Kazakhstan and Georgia to build support for its preferred pipeline route. A communiqué was signed stating support for an east–west pipeline network to carry oil and gas from the energy-rich region through Turkey to markets in the West.[58] Ankara expected pressure to intensify prior to a decision being made in October 1998 and aimed to continue to draw others to its side.[59] This decision, however, has not been taken and was continuously delayed by the international consortium in the following three years.

Another important factor related to the US and Turkish roles is Israel's involvement in the region. The then Israeli Prime Minister, Binyamin Netanyahu, has described Azerbaijan as a potential supplier of oil to Israel and has spoken favorably of a pipeline project that would enable Azerbaijan to move its crude oil across neighboring Georgia and Turkey to the northeastern corner of the Mediterranean Sea, with a prospective underwater extension to Israel. In response, Iran said Azerbaijan was playing a dangerous game and also blamed Turkey for providing Israeli access to the region.[60]

CONCLUDING OBSERVATIONS

When the idea of joint Western and Central Asian oil ventures was first proposed, Iran evinced approval, or at least acquiescence, and expressed a willingness to participate in any such venture. Indeed, Iran sought to obtain a 5 per cent share in the AIOC consortium called for under the so-called contract of the century. However, Tehran quickly saw this ambition frustrated by US pressure to exclude Iranian interests. It was the West that sought to exclude Iran from the divvying up of profits, rather than vice versa. It is this event – the inflicting of an economic wound – that one can identify as the trigger for Iran's vocal opposition to Western investment activity in the Caspian. Until mid-1997, US officials said they had no legal authority to block Iranian pipeline options. But, in autumn 1997, Washington decided to oppose allowing Iran to be a conduit for some of the world; largest untapped oil and gas reserves. Despite all these developments, Tebran's decision to join the Shakh–Deniz oil scheme shows its pragmatic stance and policy.

Iran's relations with the littoral states are subject to change should there be a setback in its relations with Russia after the recent agreement signed between Moscow and Almaty. Moscow and Tehran have been guided by a tactical friendship and need each other to counterbalance US influence in the region. The Iranian administration may have been caught by surprise by the firmness of US policy and by a changing Russian stance in the region. According to Eyup Zengin of Baku Qafqaz University, discussions on the enlargement of the European Union and the expansion of NATO are likely to foster red-brown (socialist and nationalist) factions in Russian politics that may lead to radicalization in foreign policy conduct.[61] Iran is seen as a beneficial ally by Russia and vice versa. Tehran may also develop its relations with Turkmenistan and to a lesser extent with Kazakhstan, but progress in relations with Azerbaijan is less likely due to the problems discussed above.

As Henri J. Barkey has described, after the dissolution of the Soviet Union, the Iranian regime seems to remain as the only de facto revisionist power, with limited capability, challenging the United States, the only remaining superpower in world politics.[62] Since the early years of the revolution, the Iranian leadership has seen its interests as being at odds with those of the United States. From the Iranian perspective, the United States has pursued a hostile policy toward Iran, aiming to prevent it from achieving its legitimate security and economic interests in the Middle East and adjacent regions.[63]

President Khatami expressed his desire for a dialogue between 'Iran and the great American people' in December 1997 and repeated this view in a CNN interview on 7 January 1998. Although his offer calls for an unofficial dialogue between the Iranian and American people, he raised hopes in the capitals of both the 'Great Satan' and of the 'rogue state' that the almost two-decades-old confrontation would end. From the Iranian perspective, normalization of relations with the United States would mean an immediate end to the isolation of Iran and would make possible great trade and investment prospects and open the door to the realization of the potential of the Iranian nation.[64] Rapprochement with the United States might also mean inclusion of Iran in Caspian-related projects, including possible pipelines through Iran. Resistance to some limited deals could gradually erode if positive signs continue to come from Khatami. At the same time, Washington may prefer an Iranian pipeline to Russian options. It is not a secret that the Clinton administration's executive order of May 1995 gives the US government a chance to take a positive step by encouraging oil swaps with Iran.[65] This order was designed originally to benefit landlocked former Soviet republics in the Caspian Sea region.[66] Tehran also welcomed a Clinton administration decision to waive sanctions against French, Russian and Malaysian companies involved in a $2 billion energy deal in Iran. Khatami has begun to collect the fruits of his policy of increased openness.

It is not logical to argue that Iran could at a moment's notice shut down the pipeline and thereby deprive oil-exporting countries of an important source of hard currency. In 1990, for example, Turkey shut down the oil pipeline from

Iraq to the Mediterranean and left Iraq without vital revenues. In this case, however, it was a United Nations decision and broad support from regional countries that made the closure possible.

As far as Ankara is concerned, the concept of Turkey's filling of the 'vacuum' in the Caucasus and Central Asia was generated not in Ankara or Tehran think tanks but rather in such institutions as RAND and the Heritage Foundation. These views were quickly picked up, and repeated, by influential newspapers (*New York Times, Washington Post,* and others). According to these scenarios, Turkey's move into the Muslim-inhabited former Soviet republics is meant to contain the spread of 'fundamentalist' Islamic ideas. The possibilities were greatly exaggerated if one considers Turkey's and Iran's limited capabilities and knowledge of these countries, as well as their own expectations and objectives. Both Iran and Turkey lack the resources necessary to compete for a regional leadership role in the Caucasus and Central Asia. Ignoring their intrinsic weaknesses and overestimating their strength, both Tehran and Ankara committed major mistakes in the southern area of the former Soviet Union. As Igor Lipovsky has pointed out: 'Neither Turkey nor Iran were able to take on Russia's previous role in the region.'[67]

The Central Asian countries, rather, turned toward Europe, the United States and, to some extent, the Far East. Therefore, even if there were a desire in US or European circles for competition between Turkey and Iran, they did not have a receptive audience to work with. From whatever perspective, close relations between Turkey and Iran are valuable in terms of commercial and security considerations. The United States may not welcome closer Iranian–Turkish ties, but it certainly realizes that Turkey needs to have close relations with its neighbors (especially to obtain sources for natural gas).

One may find Graham Fuller's definition of the 'center of the universe' (in his book of that name) exaggerated,[68] but Iran is certainly at the center of the newly emerging northern tier of the Middle East. Today the only country actively fighting the narcotics trade in the region is Iran, while in the other Caspian countries narcotics has in effect become part of the process of initial, generally criminal, capital accumulation. Iran's participation in Caspian Sea schemes may help it to adopt a cooperative approach and to support a constructive and peaceful climate in the region rather than adding elements of instability.

NOTES

1. *Turkmenskaya Iskra* (Russian), 8 August 1994, cited in Foreign Broadcast Information Service (FBIS), Daily Report, Near East (hereafter EBIS-NES), 14 October 1995.
2. IRNA, 11 Decemher 1995, cited in FBIS-NES, 14 December 1995.
3. Henri-Juri Uihopuu, 'The Caspian Sea: A Tangle of Legal Problems', *World Today* 51, No. 6 (June 1995); A.M. Butayev, *Kaspiyi more ili ozero?* (Is Caspian a sea or lake?), Mahackala, 1998.

4. *Third UN Conference on the Law of the Sea, UN Convention on the Law of the Sea*, UN Doc. A/Conf.62/122 (New York: United Nations, 1982).
5. Ibid., Article 3.
6. Ibid., Article 57.
7. 'Turkmen–Azeri Oulfield Dispute Remains Unresolved', BBC Summary of World Broadcasts, 8 August 1997.
8. 'Russia's Caspian Oil Riches May Prove Illusory', BBC Summary of World Broadcasts, 27 June 1997.
9. Aleksander Akimov, 'Oil and Gas in the Caspian Sea Region: An Overview of Cooperation and Conflict', *Perspectives on Central Asia* (June 1996) at http://www.cpss.org'easianw/akim.txt.
10. Yuri Federov, 'Russia's Policies toward Caspian Region Oil: Neo-Imperial or Pragmatic?' *Perspectives on Central Asia* (September 1996) at http://www.cpss.org/casianw/setpers.html.
11. Mikbail Peresvezbin, 'Ashkabad "Trio" Ready to Become Quintet', *Russian Press Digest*, 14 November 1996, p.3.
12. *Financial Times*, 7 July 1998.
13. Andrei Sboumikbin, 'Economics and Politics of Developing Caspian Oil Resources', *Perspectives on Central Asia* (November 1996) at http://www.cpss.org/casianw/novpers.html.
14. 'Iranian Foreign Ministry Says Bilateral Pacts over Caspian Not Acceptable', BBC Summary of World Broadcasts, MF/D3274/MED, 9 July 1998.
15. Liz Fuller, 'The Caspian Pipeline Tug of War', *OMRI Program Brief* (Prague), 3 October 1995.
16. Malik Mufti, 'Dacing and Caution in Turkish Foreign Policy', *Middle East Journal* 52, No. 1 (Winter 1998).
17. Gussein Baguirov, personal correspondence with the author, 15 April 1998.
18. *Turan*, 30 June 94, cited in FBIS, *Daily Report, Central Eurasia* (hereafter FBIS-SOV), 12 October 1995.
19. *Turan*, 6 July 94, cited in FBIS-SOV, 12 October 1995.
20. *Azadlyg* (Azeri), 12 July 94, p.6, cited in FBIS-SOV; 12 October 1995.
21. *Rossiyskaya Gazeta* (Russian), 2 February 1995, 6, cited in FBIS-SOV; 19 October 1995.
22. IRNA, 28 January 1995, cited in FBIS-NES, 19 October 1995.
23. *Turkish Daily News*, 18 October 1995, p.A4.
24. Interfax, 13 February 1995, cited in FBIS-SOV, 19 October 1995.
25. *Salam* (Persian), 15 February 1995, p.2, cited in FBIS-NFS, 18 October 1995.
26. *Jomhuri-ye Eslami* (Persian), 9 April 1995, p.2, cited in FEIS-NFS, 14 October 1995
27. Interfax, 9 December 1995, cited in FBIS-SOV, 14 December 1995.
28. *Turan*, 14 December 1995, cited in FBIS-SOV, 18 December 1995.
29. Interfax, 10 May 1996, cited in FBIS-SOV, 30 May 1997; Aleksey Comov, 'Neftnovogo veka' (Oil of New Century), *Neft Rossii*, No. 10 (1997), p.5
30. Interfax, 2 February 1995, cited in FBIS-SOV, 19 November 1995.
31. *Karavan* (Russian), 16 April 1996, p.3, cited in FBIS-SOV, 12 June 1996.
32. Interfax, 16 May 1996, cited in FEIS-SOV, 3 June 1997.
33. IRNA, 11 May 1996, cited in FBJS-NES, 30 May 1998.
34. ITAR-TASS, 18 January 1997, cited in FBIS-SOV, 23 January 1997.
35. Phil Reeves, 'Allies Risk US Ire over Tehran Oil Deal', *Independent,* 14 May 1997, p.8.
36. ITAR-TASS, 8 October 1994, cited in FBIS-SOV, 12 November 1995.
37. IRNA, 25 October 1994, cited in FBIS-SOV, 11 November 1995
38. IRNA, 28 February 1995, cited in FBIS-NES, 18 November 1995.
39. Mehmet Turna, personal correspondence with the author, 20 March 1998.
40. IRNA, 17 March 1997, cited in FBIS-SOV, 19 March 1997.
41. G. Starchenkov, 'Is the Caspian Going to Be a Sea of Discord?' *Aziya i Afrika Segodriya* (Russian), No. 12 (December 1994), pp.15–18, cited in FB1S-SOV, 18 November 1995.
42. *Noyan Tapan*, 14 November 1995, cited in FBIS-SOV, 19 November 1995.
43. IRNA, 7 March 1996, cited in FBIS-SOV, 25 March 1998.
44. *Turkmen Press* (Russian), 27 March 96, cited in FBIS-SOV, 16 April 1998.
45. Voice of the Islamic Republic of Iran, Tehran, 23 January 1996, cited in FBIS-NES, 25 January 1996.
46. ITAR-TASS, 13 November 1996, cited in FBIS-SOV, 14 November 1996.
47. IRNA, 13 October 1997, cited in FBIS-NES, 15 October 1997.

51

48. Interfax, 13 November 1996, cited in FBIS-SOV, 15 November 1996.
49. Interfax, 14 November 1996, cited in FBIS-SOV, 18 November 1996.
50. David E. Sanger, 'White House Woos Turkinenistan's Chief', *New York Times*, 24 April 1998.
51. For two recent comprehensive articles on the US policy toward the Caspian region, see Michael P. Croissant, 'U.S. Interests in the Caspian Sca Basin', *Comparative Strategy*, No. 16 (Autumn 1997); and S. Frederick Starr, 'Power Failure: American Policy in the Caspian', *National Interest*, No. 47 (Spring 1997).
52. *Turan*, 11 March 1995, cited in FBIS-SOV, 18 November 1995.
53. IRNA, 13 June 1995, cited in FBIS-NES, 14 November 1995.
54. *Iran News*, 8 April 1995, cited in FBIS-SOV, 14 November 1995.
55. IRNA, 8 January 1996, cited in FBIS-NES, 22 January 1996.
56. *Nokta* (Istanbul), 5–11 March 1995, 22-4.
57. Botas official, confidential personal correspondence with the author, 27 February 1998.
58. John Barham, 'Turkey Builds Pipeline Accord', *Financial Times*, 3 March 1998, p.4.
59. Turkish petroleum official, confidential personal correspondence with the author, 5 March 1998.
60. Bülent Aras, 'Post-Cold War Realities: Israel's Strategy in Azerhaijan and Central Asia', *Middle East Policy* 5, No. 2 (January 1998, pp.68–81.
61. Eyup Zengin, dean of Economics and Administrative Sciences Department, Qafqaz University, Azerbaijan, personal correspondence with the author, 15 April 1998.
62. Henri J. Barkey, 'Iran and Turkey: Confrontation across an Ideological Divide', in Alvin Z. Ruhinstein and Oles M. Smolansky (eds), *Regional Power Rivalries in the New Eurasia: Russia, Turkey, and Iran*, (Armonk, NY: M. F. Sharpe, 1995), p.148.
63. R. K. Ramazani, 'Iran; Foreign Policy: Both North and South', *Middle East Journal* 46, No. 3 (Summer 1992); and *idem*, 'The Shifting Premise of Iran's Foreign Policy: Towards a Democratic Peace', *Middle East Journal* 52, No. 2 (Spring 1998).
64. Jahangir Amuzegar, 'Iran under New Management', *SAIS Review* 18, No. 1 (Spring 1998); and Gary Sick, 'Rethinking Dual Containment', *Survival* 40, No. 1 (Spring 1998).
65. 'Meeting the Iranian Challenge', *Journal of Commerce*, 16 April 1998, p.6A.
66. Policy analyst, US Department of State, confidenhal interview with the author, Washington, DC, 6–8 April 1998.
67. Igor P. Lipovsky, 'Central Asia: In Search of a New Political Identity', *Middle East Journal* 50, No. 2 (Spring 1996).
68. Graham Fuller, *Center of the Universe* (Boulder, CO: Westview, 1991).

4

ISRAEL'S STRATEGY IN AZERBAIJAN AND CENTRAL ASIA

The rapidly shifting balances of the 1990s and new developments stemming from the acceleration of economic globalization have forced Israel to re-evaluate and reshape its foreign-policy strategy. The tactical phases of Israel's new strategy are as follows: 1) to solve its border conflicts and to form a security belt within the peace process; 2) to conclude the process of integration and recognition as a legitimate and equal state in its region in this security belt; 3) to gain diplomatic flexibility in manipulating the interstate conflicts of the Middle Eastern countries; 4) to exploit the resources of the region and introduce multicountry projects with the support of international Jewish communities; 5) after gaining legitimacy in the region, to open up Asia and then to develop its diplomatic and economic relations with the more southern countries; 6) to use the opportunities created by the complex web of relations mentioned above to reach an influential position in the formation of global strategies and to escape from the confines of the Middle East to establish a greater global presence.[1]

This is not Israel's first attempt to create a sphere of influence in the Greater Middle East region. In the 1950s, the Israeli leader David Ben-Gurion sought to generate a non-Arab Middle Eastern alliance which would have consisted of Turkey, Ethiopia, Iran and Israel. This attempt, called a 'periphery strategy', ultimately failed because of the fall of the Iranian Shah in the late 1970s.[2] Since then, however, Israel has sought to develop ties to any 'moderate' Muslim country willing to assist Israel in the effort to undercut its anti-Muslim image, or the perception that all Muslim countries are allied against it. After the lessons learned from earlier attempts, Israel has introduced a more comprehensive vision as part of its new strategy to gain greater influence in the region, with special emphasis on the new republics of Central Asia.

THE SOURCE OF THE MUTUAL INTERESTS

With the collapse of the Soviet Union, several new republics became a part of the Middle East due to their status as Muslim countries. These Central Asian states appeared on the agenda of the Israeli administration even before they had won their independence from Moscow. Israel's surprisingly early contacts and developing relations with these republics are evidence of the importance attached to this region.

One goal of these early attempts has been to set a barrier against the expansion of Arab and Iranian influence in the new republics. The main aim has been to pre-empt the threat of 'Islamic fundamentalism'. Early attempts by some Arab countries to draw Central Asian states into the Arab–Israeli conflict worried Israel,[3] which has tried to counter the inherent advantages of the Arabs and Iran stemming from their cultural and religious closeness to the people of Central Asia. Even if such a scenario were possible, the dominant tendency in Central Asian states has been to avoid involvement in the struggles of the Middle East.[4]

The Palestinian Liberation Organization's (PLO) diplomatic push in the Central Asian republics to mobilize support for the Palestinian cause has exaggerated the situation in the eyes of the Israeli administration. Yasser Arafat's visit to Kazakhstan in January 1992 led to its recognition of the Palestinian state. The two sides agreed on the highest level of representation, stimulating Israel to take measures in response. The former Israeli Prime Minister Yitzhak Shamir wrote letters to 23 members of the US Congress urging them to use their influence to persuade Kazakhstan to diminish the closeness of its relations with the Palestinians. At the same time, the Israeli government attempted to push the then US Secretary of State James A. Baker III to warn Kazakhstan to reconsider its relations with the PLO.[5] Despite these provisions, the PLO maintained its presence in the new Central Asian states. In February 1992, Arafat's visit to Uzbekistan was announced, and in March, Tajikistan extended diplomatic relations to the PLO.[6]

In April 1992, an Uzbek delegate visited Saudi Arabia and participated in a conference which called for the recognition of the legitimate rights of the Palestinian people and a just solution to the Palestinian question. After this event, a conference on the Dagestan–Israel Friendship Society was canceled due to possible Muslim reaction which might have injured relations with some Middle Eastern states.[7]

However, thanks to certain advantages possessed by Israel, these attempts have not prevented its penetration of Central Asia. Israel's powerful image promises much to these countries, which perceive it as a model state: small but politically and economically strong, and both democratic and secular.[8] Despite the general rule that the Central Asian republics have strong leaders and weak democracies, they have almost uniformly given special weight to developing relations with democratic countries. Israel follows a pragmatic approach in establishing relationships with Muslim regimes whether democratic or authoritarian. In this respect, the governments of the new Central Asian states all agree that Israel, with its technological skills and democratic example, may ease the integration of these new republics into the modern world system. In addition, Israel is perceived in many countries as a gateway to the Western world in general, and to the US in particular.[9]

The last advantage of Israel, mostly overlooked in academic circles, carries important implications. The new Central Asian states are so poor economically that they are willing to accept financial assistance from any state that extends it, in the form of investment or of direct aid. The Central Asian states have thus welcomed Israeli assistance, and the consequent rapidly developing relations have become clear evidence of Israel's increasingly extensive ties in the enlarged Middle East.[10]

RELATIONS WITH THE US, TURKEY AND RUSSIA

Three important Israeli political maneuvers were required for Israel's new strategy with respect to the emerging Central Asian republics. First, Israel has been forced to reshape its policy toward the United Sates. In the aftermath of the Cold War, the strategic environment that led the United States to place a priority on relations with Israel has changed dramatically. The role Israel had assumed in the Middle East vis-à-vis the Soviet Union is no longer valid. Thus Israel has been prompted to attempt to carve out a new security niche: it has focused its sights on the states of Central Asia and the Caucasus.[11] The Israeli plan seems to be to take advantage of US support for its steps in the Central Asian republics.

In August 1992, the United States and Israel introduced a joint project in these republics, with the United States putting up the required financing and Israel providing technology transfer and expertise in certain other areas. In addition, the trumpeting of an Islamic fundamentalist threat in Central Asia by conservative circles in the US seems targeted at the Western, particularly the US, audience. As is well known, Western regimes are heavily partial to secular societies. The so-called 'power vacuum' in Central Asia has encouraged Israel's attempt to promote Western styles of government in this region.[12]

Israel's second political maneuver has been to form an alliance with Turkey. The collapse of the USSR has created as much of a window of opportunity for the Turkish administration as for the Israeli. The emergence of new states in Central Asia has caused a radical shift in the foreign policy of Turkey and has triggered a search for means of tactical political-economic penetration into the new Central Asian republics.[13] The efforts of Turkish policy makers have been motivated by the desire to spread the Turkish model: parliamentary democracy, a relatively free-market economy and secularism in an Islamic society. The resurgence of the Turkic world has provided Turkey with the opportunity to regain its earlier geostrategic significance.

Turkey and Israel are not the only Middle Eastern actors involved in the establishment of spheres of influence in the Central Asian and Caucasian region.[14] Iran and Saudi Arabia have also moved to improve their relations with the countries in the area, a development that has paved the way to implicit cooperation between Israel and Turkey as a result of their shared secularist stance. In the words of an Israeli foreign-policy expert: 'The perception in Washington of an anti-American Islamic threat in the Middle East and Central Asia has produced another marketing formula for Israel. With Turkey, which like Israel appears to have lost its strategic value to the West as a result of the end of the Cold War, trying to sell itself as a new pro-American "pillar" against Islamic fundamentalism, the idea of an Israeli–Turkish alliance has been integrated into the Israeli post-cold war strategy vis-à-vis Washington.'[15]

Turkey has always been well aware of Israel's strong support in the United States and Israel has been sympathetic toward Turkey due to the historically tolerant attitude of the Ottoman Empire toward the Jews. And, of course, they are both non-Arab states on the periphery of the Arab world.

It should be added that the prospect of cooperation between Israel and Turkey with respect to the new republics has been limited to setting up barriers to the development of fundamentalism, making joint investments in agriculture and related sectors, and jointly contributing to the construction of some training facilities. Both countries know that they cannot offer a panacea for all the political and economic ills of Central Asia.

What cooperation has occurred, however, is significant from the perspectives of both countries. From Israel's point of view, cooperation with Turkey may neutralize some problems in its attempts to penetrate into the markets of the former Soviet republics. In addition, Turkey is seen as a natural ally in Israel's struggle against Iran. The visit by Turkey's then Prime Minister, Tansu Çiller, to Israel in autumn 1994 was indicative of the perceived importance of Israel to Turkey's interests. One of the main subjects on the negotiating table was investment in the Central Asian states. Moscow radio pointed out that Turkish and Israeli officials aim to make joint investments in the former Soviet republics ranging from agriculture to environmental protection and further stated that 'these projects promise much to all sides'.[16] In December 1996, representatives of 30 Israeli and 100 Turkish firms came together and discussed joint projects in the Central Asian republics.[17]

Perhaps the best evidence of the irreversibility of the improved relations between Turkey and Israel is the fact that the former neo-conservative and Islamist Erbakan government of Turkey, which had previously adopted a hard line, declared that it was not against close relations and signed several agreements with Israel in 1996 despite Arab resistance.[18] In the first half of 1997, a series of agreements – most related to military cooperation – were added to the prior ones.[19] According to press reports, Turkish military circles are in favor of closer relations with Israel, and several high-ranking military staff members visited Israel in the first months of 1997.[20] Then deputy chief of the

Turkish General Staff, Cevik Bir, argued that 'Turkey and Israel are the two democratic countries in the region, and we must show the region that democracies can work together'.[21] Turkey's President Suleyman Demirel also underlined the importance of Israeli–Turkish cooperation for the security and stability of the Middle East in an interview published recently in *Al-Wasat*.[22]

It is obvious that the dynamics of the post-Soviet era in the Middle East have drawn Israel, Turkey and the United States under the same interest umbrella.[23] Further illustrative of this conjuncture is the fact that, on 31 October 1994, these three countries inaugurated a new agriculture project in Uzbekistan and Turkmenistan.[24] At the time, this enterprise was endorsed by Marc Grossman, the US ambassador to Ankara, who declared that 'there is a great potential in the US–Turkish–Israeli assistance program in Central Asia'.[25] Israel clearly aims to maintain American support while planning to diversify its own foreign-policy prerogatives at a time when the Arab nations are preoccupied with peace negotiations with Israel.

Russia is a third force that has represented a potential obstacle to expanded Israeli presence in the new republics of Central Asia. The former superpower borders on the new republics and has traditionally played a paramount role in the politics and economics of the region. During the period following the collapse of the Soviet Union, the countries of Eurasia took on a position of primary importance for Russian foreign-policy objectives. Therefore, not surprisingly, the Russian far right has strongly opposed Israel's involvement in Central Asia: 'Among the advocates of this position was the clearly anti-Semitic and anti-Israeli Vladimir Zhrinovsky, who had placed third in the presidential elections of June 1991.'[26] Israel has been aware that Russia could make much mischief, and so has not been willing to go too far to provoke Moscow. It has been careful not to join forces with any power that might be perceived as a threat to Moscow's core interests in its own backyard.

As seen in discussions concerning NATO's expansion, Russia has not been ready to accept a Western alliance that would come right up to its borders, a prospect it perceives as a threat.[27] Israel and Turkey both fear that NATO's expansion may provoke Russia to act more aggressively in its 'near abroad' and to exceed the limits established by the Conventional Forces in Europe (CFE) treaty.[28] In this delicate atmosphere, the Israeli Prime Minister, Binyamin Netanyahu, paid a visit to Moscow on 11 March 1997. He discussed bilateral relations and the Middle East peace process with President Yeltsin, Prime Minister Chernomyrdin and Foreign Minister Yevgeni Primakov. Netanyahu expressed concern regarding Russia's escalating technical and military cooperation with Iran and Syria, arguing that it threatened regional stability.[29]

According to Sergei Arutiunov, a prominent Russian political scientist, at this point the negative consequences of a joint Israeli–Turkish move in Central Asia may greatly outweigh the potentially limited positive results. He argues further that:

> a Turco-Israeli close cooperation is a positive fact from the world-wide point of view. But generally it would worsen Russian–Turkish and Russian–Israeli relations. It also may provoke the re-emerging anti-Semitism in Russia. It will evoke much of anxiety in Armenia, too. First a mutually acceptable solution about Karabagh must be found and only then a Turkish–Israeli cooperation may start to be realized in the Near East and the former USSR states. Otherwise it may trigger Russian–Iraqi, Russian–Iranian, Armenian–Iranian rapproachments [sic], push Armenian extremists in the world to a cooperation with Palestinian extremists.[30]

ISRAEL AND CENTRAL ASIAN REPUBLICS

Initially, the Israeli administration gave priority to diplomacy and trade over utilizing domestic Jewish influence in the new republics of Central Asia, despite the fact that some of these countries have substantial Jewish populations.[31] Thus by the end of 1992, Israel had granted official recognition to Azerbaijan, Kazakhstan, Kirgyzstan and Tajikistan. Finally, Israel established diplomatic relations with Turkmenistan in 1993.

However, since the independence of Azerbaijan and other former Soviet republics, Jewish friendship societies have accelerated Israeli penetration of the region. In the 1990s, due to increased migration, relations between Soviet Jews and Israelis have grown stronger, and different Israeli organizations have intensified their activities in post-Soviet Central Asia. For example, in March 1992, the Jewish Agency prepared a conference on the Israeli economic experience in Tashkent. In June, an Azerbaijan–Israel friendship society convened a meeting in Haifa and called for support for the Azerbaijani administration in its struggle against Armenia. The same foundation later organized activities during an important Jewish religious festival. In September of the same year, the Jewish Agency organized a summer camp for children from Kazakhstan and Kirgyzstan.[32] In the meantime, Israel has appointed an ambassador to Uzbekistan, its first to any Central Asian republic.

Azerbaijan

As discussed above, Israel established diplomatic relations with Azerbaijan early on, causing much consternation in some countries. Indeed, the Iranian media often criticize Turkey for helping Israel establish diplomatic relations with Azerbaijan.[33] Since then, Israel has attempted to play an active role in the affairs of Azerbaijan, both economically and militarily.[34] For example, it took a decisive stance on the Azerbaijani side in the Nagorno-Karabakh conflict. According to some sources, both Israel and Turkey have supplied arms and military equipment to Azerbaijan.[35] Although the purchase of stinger missiles was denied by the Azerbaijan Defense Ministry, speculations on arms transfer continue.

As an analytical review of Turan News Agency argued, 'Israel is always perceived in Azerbaijan as a potential strategic partner, and at times a sense of bewilderment has been expressed that their cooperation is developing too slowly.'[36] As Sule Kut points out, Azerbaijani officials attach special importance to Israel. The number of Israeli businessmen in Azerbaijan and Central Asian countries has reached several hundred. She further argues that 'according to Azerbaijani officials Israel as a secular, democratic and militarily powerful western country may be a threat to the Middle Eastern states. But it is an opportunity for Azerbaijan'.[37] The Azeri government also pursues good relations with Jews living in Azerbaijan. President Heidar Aliyev visits the Tats' (as many Azerbaijani Jews call themselves) Synagogue and his portrait hangs in its office.[38]

In March 1992, direct charter flights between Azerbaijan and Israel became regular. The first official Azeri visit to Israel took place in September 1992. During official talks, cooperation on politics, economy, science and culture was on the table.[39] Israel opened an embassy in Baku in February 1993.

According to the Iranian News Agency (IRNA), an Israeli intelligence delegation arrived in Baku in August 1995. IRNA described the visit as a secret mission to train Azerbaijani security agents.[40] The Azerbaijani National Security Ministry denied these allegations and noted that it was prepared to openly develop cooperation with the special services of many other countries.[41] The Israeli Health Minister, Efraim Sene, suggested that 'Israel has a strategic interest in developing ties with Azerbaijan, which is equally interested in such ties because they can help stem the onset of Islamic fundamentalism emanating from Iran'.[42] Lowell Bezanis agrees with this point and further argues that 'Azerbaijan's interest in Israel, and vice versa, stems from their mutual fear of Iran. In cultivating ties with Israel, Azerbaijan also wishes to win plaudits from the US'.[43] This cooperation may also be regarded as an effort to hold off Russian pressure and to counter Iran's growing ties to Armenia and Georgia. In this line of thinking, Eliezer Yotvat, Israel's first ambassador to Azerbaijan, said that he has succeeded in raising Israeli–Azerbaijani relations 'from zero ... to a high level'.[44] In the first four months of 1996, Israeli exports to Azerbaijan amounted to roughly \$3.5 million.[45]

Israel's Prime Minister, Binyamin Netanyahu, on his way back to Israel from his visit to Japan and South Korea, stopped briefly in Baku and met with the President of Azerbaijan, Heidar Aliyev, on 29 August 1997. Netanyahu noted how much these two states have in common as follows:

We are two ancient peoples who have achieved independence in the last decades and now the task for us as independent nations is to continue to develop our countries ... I also find great hope in that fact that we have relationship as we do with Turkey, with Jordan, with Egypt, between the Jewish state and predominantly Muslim states ... This gives us hope that all the children of Abraham can find peace and friendship under the same sun that rises over the Caspian sea and sets over Mediterranean.[46]

Aliyev said Azerbaijan wanted to tap Israeli technological expertise. Netanyahu reiterated his concern about possible sales of nuclear technology to his country's arch foe, Iran, which shares a long land and sea border with Azerbaijan.47 Furthermore, Netanyahu described Azerbaijan as a potential supplier of oil to Israel and emphasized a pipeline project that would enable Azerbaijan to move its crude oil across neighboring Georgia and Turkey to the northeastern corner of the Mediterranean Sea and a prospective underwater extension to Israel. Netanyahu said: 'We are involved in this project ... It will enable us to buy oil at a much lower price.'[48]

Netanyahu evidently discussed the feasibility of three-sided cooperation between Israel, Turkey and Azerbaijan in stemming the tide of Islamic fanaticism emanating from Iran. Iran's state radio the next day blasted Azerbaijan for hosting the Israeli Prime Minister, saying: 'Baku has been playing a dangerous game by receiving the Zionist regime's expansionist prime minister. By doing this it has destabilised its own ties with Islamic states in the region and the world.'[49] The Armenian Foreign Minister, Alexander Arzumanyan, also considered the close cooperation between Turkey and Israel to be extremely dangerous for the region, saying that it was even more dangerous for Azerbaijan to join them. He underlined the importance of Tehran–Yerevan ties at a time when regional cooperation was rapidly expanding.[50] It seems particularly important for Israel to firm up its partnership along the axis of Turkey and Azerbaijan to compensate Baku. Economic assistance is not enough in this regard. Azerbaijan's main expectation is Israeli assistance along the lines of political lobbying

Shimon Stein, the deputy director of the Israeli Foreign Ministry department for the CIS and Central Europe, said during a visit to Baku in January 1999 that the potential exists for developing economic links between Azerbaijan and Israel. He noted that Israel supports the Baku–Ceyhan route for the main oil pipeline as it was advantageous for the entire Transcaucasus from both the economic and strategic angles. The project will put an end to Azerbaijan's dependence on other countries, according to Stein.[51] President Aliyev had chosen the Israeli aircraft industries to modernize his Topolev presidential aircraft at the Bet Shemesh plant, near Tel Aviv, and invited Turkish and Israeli security experts to train his private guard units.[52]

Tajikistan

Like Azerbaijan, Tajikistan has attracted the attention of many investors with its rich raw materials and plentiful human resources. While this country once seemed attractive to Israel as a target for investment, interest waned with the outbreak of civil war in Tajikistan at the end of the 1992. However, Israel has still maintained active diplomatic ties, and there has been some activity on the economic front. Israel's ambassador to Russia was given the responsibility for Tajikistan. In February 1992, an Israeli delegate traveled to Tajikistan and signed an agreement for the transferal of Israeli expertise in agriculture and the exploitation of Tajik crude oil.

Islamic elements claim to play an important role in politics in Tajikistan, and even briefly attained control of the government. However, the Muslim authority in Tajikistan, Akbar Turajanzade, has said that he would not oppose Israeli–Tajik diplomatic relations. Despite this claim, the banners 'Death to the US, Death to Israel' were in evidence during demonstrations in April 1992.[53] In response, a number of Israeli business delegates visited Tajikistan to impress upon the government that there is nothing to fear from the Israeli state.[54] In August, Ambassador Arya Levin was welcomed in Dushanbe by President Nabiyev. The Tajik President has invited Israeli business people to his country.[55]

Uzbekistan

Israel has had a more substantial relationship with Uzbekistan, the dissemination of irrigation technology forming its core. In September 1992, Israel's Beta Shita company signed an agreement for the construction of a high-technology irrigation scheme in the Andezhan region. The same company has also invested in Turkmenistan and Tajikistan.[56] The Akkurgan demonstration farm is another promising project. It is one of the agricultural demonstration activities established under the special cooperation program developed in the Central Asian Republics by MASHAV, the Center for International Cooperation of the Israel Ministry of Foreign Affairs, in cooperation with the US Agency for International Development (USAID). The MASHAV–USAID Program aims to address key agricultural issues and promote economic endeavors, as well as international cooperation. It reflects Israel's commitment to share with others appropriate technologies, know-how, human-resource training and practical experience gained in agricultural and rural development.[57] Training activities were conducted in both Israel and Uzbekistan.

Israel has also been exporting its expertise in cotton production to Uzbekistan. According to a *Financial Times* report in May 1992, the Israeli projects in Uzbekistan have increased cotton output by 30 per cent while

61

reducing water consumption by two-thirds.[58] The Foreign Trade Relations Minister of Uzbekistan, Sadik Safayev, notes that a total of four Israeli companies deal regularly with Uzbekistan.[59]

Turkmenistan

Israel and Turkmenistan have had diplomatic relations since 1993. This late recognition, however, did not prevent the development of economic relations prior to that date. In the summer of 1992, an Israeli business delegation visited Turkmenistan to offer a number of projects in agricultural technology and rural development.[60] However, the cost of irrigation and desalination projects alone were expected to exceed $10 billion, and, as it would be difficult for the Turkmen government to raise this amount, it has not yet agreed to the project. The most convenient solution would be a barter agreement.

Since official recognition in 1993, economic cooperation has increased. In 1994, Turkmenistan's Deputy Prime Minister visited Jerusalem and Israel's Shimon Peres visited Ashkhabad. Numerous cooperation accords have been signed. The US–Israel joint project on education and technology transfer in agriculture can be taken as an important sign of development.[61] The volume of trade between Turkmenistan and Israel exceeded $40 million in 1995.[62] In addition, in March 1995, Turkmenistan and Israel signed an agreement on cooperation in health care, under which Israel will provide assistance to Turkmenistan in child and maternity care, medical insurance, organization of ambulance services and supply of medical equipment.[63] The Israeli firm Ben Shanar Associates currently extends financial services in Turkmenistan, Uzbekistan and Kazakhstan.[64]

On 25 May 1995, the Turkmen leader, Turkmenbashi Saparmurad Niyazov, traveled to Israel, where he met with his Israeli counterpart, Ezer Weizman, as well as with Prime Minister Yitzhak Rabin and Foreign Minister Shimon Peres for talks focusing on bilateral economic relations. Israel is involved in a $100 million irrigation project and a scheme to build a gas pipeline to Turkey from that country, which has some of the world's largest gas reserves.[65] Executives at Merhav, an Israeli company invested in Turkmenistan, believe it is possible for the pipeline to be extended to Israel.[66]

Merhav also signed a $500 million contract to upgrade the Turkmenbashi refinery in Turkmenistan in August 1996. The project is aimed at improving two units, a Continuous Catalytic Reforming and Fluid Catalytic Cracker, and financing a third new unit for processing lubricating oil.[67] The representative of Merhav, Yosej A. Maiman, was seen frequently on Turkmen television with Turkmenbashi, and Turkmen media pay special attention to the activities of Maiman's company.[68]

Kazakhstan

Israel enjoys widespread influence in Kazakhstan. At first, its roughly one million German-origin population worried Israel, but any difficulties were soon overcome with diplomatic and economic maneuvers. Israel, like other countries, first offered agriculture-related projects. The most active Israeli companies to date have been Beta Shita, Netafim and Merhav.[69] In February 1992, four different projects were signed targeting tomato and cotton production, and these have reportedly multiplied tomato yields sixfold.[70]

Then, in October 1992, an additional series of agreements was accepted by the two countries,[71] following which Israel's Lachist firm made significant investments. Its Davy Foundation project is the largest known initiative in agriculture and animal husbandry to date. In a short time, this project has increased milk production by 60 per cent while reducing costs considerably.[72] Besides agriculture, Israel has invested in other sectors, from banking to supermarkets.

Kazakhstan has welcomed the positive developments in the Palestinian–Israeli peace process. The Kazakh Foreign Ministry issued a statement that: 'positive changes in the Middle East leading to peaceful settlement of the Arab–Israeli conflict should become irreversible in the interests of establishing mutual confidence, developing broad economic cooperation in the region and creating an integral security system in Asia'.[73]

The Kazakh leader, Nursultan Nazarbayev, visited Israel in December 1995. During talks held with the Israeli Foreign Minister, Ehud Baraq, he said that they 'share Israel's stand on the Iranian issue and work to prevent Iranian influence in Kazakhstan'.[74]

Israel plans to build Kazakhstan's telecommunications network. Israel is the only country in the Middle East with a comparative advantage in telecommunications equipment. The two states have already agreed on a project that includes technology transfers in telephone, telex and telegraph. Israel has also established direct satellite and telegraph connection to Uzbekistan. Since the visit of the Kazakh Prime Minister Terescenko to Israel, direct flights between the countries have become regular.

Kirghyzstan

The final country in this discussion is the Kirghyz Republic. Its President, Asker Akayev, recognized Israel during a visit in January 1993. Despite the protests of some Muslim countries, Akayev moved further and opened an embassy in Jerusalem. In this respect, Kirghyzstan's apparently positive relations with Israel have disturbed Iran and some other countries. Despite this disapproval, relations continue between the two countries. The Israeli and Kirghyz governments have agreed to cooperate on a wide range of areas including media, science, technology, cultural activities and joint-venture investments. Additionally, Israel has already supplied an important part of the debt requirement of the public and private sectors in Kirghyzstan.[75]

THE ROLES OF IRAN AND TURKEY

It is clear that Israeli attempts to enter into the Central Asian states and Azerbaijan should not be disregarded. Israel's efforts to date seem to be the most advantageous formula for a country that aims to create for itself a sphere of influence in Central Asia. It appears that Israel is the only country in the region with the necessary expertise to offer these new states. Israeli involvement in improving the telecommunications sectors of the Central Asian states shows its seriousness.

This is not to ignore the fact that Arab states and Iran have also offered financial aid and investment in certain areas, in addition to their cultural activities. The role of Iran in the region in particular is sure to be a significant one over time, as it is difficult to imagine a stable and secure Middle East without Iran. But the role of Iran is an evolving one. Indeed, there have been increasing signs that a change is taking place in relations between Israel and Iran.

A short time after the 1995 election, Tehran discerned a moderation in Israeli declarations toward Iran and Islam. In his early speeches, the Israeli leader Netanyahu claimed that Israel had no dispute with Islam. Netanyahu relaxed the political pressure against Iran, and in November 1996 he used Germany's Chancellor Kohl as a conduit to Iran to ask President Rafsanjani to prevent terrorist attacks in Israel.[76]

Turkey also can assist Iran to improve its relations with the Western world.[77] Turkey's developing relations with Israel should increase its leverage both in regard to Israel and with respect to Turkey's adversaries. What is more, in this intense competition in the so-called 'new great game', Israel and Turkey should play exemplary roles in cooperating to improve democracy and economic performance in the enlarged Middle East.[78]

The existence of nuclear weapons and technology in Central Asia worries Israel and increases the strategic importance of the region. Israel's fear stems from the possibility of the transfer of nuclear weapons and technology to Iran. According to a report prepared in France, the Mossad and the CIA keep a close eye on the nuclear-energy experts of the Central Asian states.[79] Moscow's own readiness to sell two nuclear reactors to Iran while insisting that they would not be used for military purposes worries Israel.

In addition, the possibility of the installation of Russian S-300 surface-to-air missiles in Greek Cyprus could endanger not only Turkey but also Israel's freedom of action in the eastern Mediterranean.[80] According to press reports, as tension over the possible transfer of Russian S-300 missiles to Greek

Cyprus escalates, the US, Israel and Azerbaijan are contacting Turkey to provide intelligence concerning which methods might be used for the transportation of missiles.[81] This situation forces Israel and Turkey to develop new security initiatives. Neither country should ignore the possibility that 'any hand overplayed by Turkey and Israel, together with the US, could encourage Moscow to attempt to revive its fortunes as a great power by again playing patron to the more radical states in the region'.[82]

CONCLUSION

In sum, Israel is now an integral part of the new and enlarged Middle East. It is trying to develop a new, coherent and innovative foreign policy toward the area through its focus on the Central Asian republics. It has succeeded in reconciling its short-term political maneuvers with its long-term strategy. It seems to have reached its one main aspiration of the Cold War era: an economic hinterland. Aware of the need to avoid upsetting crucial strategic balances, Israel has attempted to direct its Central Asian policy in cooperation with the US and Turkey.

NOTES

1. Ahmet Davutoglu, 'Yahudi Meselesinin Tarihi Donusumu ve Israil'in Yeni Stratejisi' (The Historical Transformation of the Jewish Question and the New Isaeli Strategy), *Avrasya Dosyasi* 1, No. 3 (Autumn 1994), pp.66–7.
2. Philip Robins, 'The Middle East and Central Asia', in Peter Ferdinand (ed.), *The New Central Asia and Its Neighbours* (London: Royal Institute, 1994), p.96.
3. Anoushiravan Ehtesami and Emma C. Murphy, 'The Non-Arab Middle East States and the Caucasian/Central Asian Republics: Iran and Israel', *International Relations* 12, No.1 (April 1994), p.96.
4. Olcott opposes this view and argues that Central Asian states accept the premise that relations with Israel must remain hostile for the sake of obtaining assistance from rich Arabian states. See Martha Brill Olcott, *Central Asia's New States* (Washington: USIP, 1996), pp.32–3.
5. Leon T. Hadar, 'The Last Days of Likud: The American–Israeli Big Chill', *Journal of Palestine Studies* 21, No.4 (Summer 1992), pp.87–8.
6. Personal interview with Officials in the Embassy of Palestine in Turkey, 17 March 1997.
7. Anoushiravan Ehteshami, 'New Frontiers: Iran, the GCC, and the CCARs', in Anoushiravan Ehtesami (ed.), *From the Gulf to Central Asia: Players in the New Great Game* (Exeter: University of Exeter Press, 1994), p.96; Reha Yilmaz, Director of the Daghestan Research Center (Derbent-Daghestan), argues that the Jewish population in Daghestan continues to migrate to Israel and that friendship socities try to accelerate this process (personal correspondence).
8. Ehteshami and Murphy, 'The Non-Arab Middle East', p.96.
9. Raphael Israeli, 'Return to the Source: The Republics of Central Asia and the Return of the Middle East', *Central Asian Survey* 13, No. 1 (1994), p.29.
10. Anthony Hyman, 'Central Asia and the Middle East: The Emerging Links', in Mohiaddin Mesbahi (ed.), *Central Asia and the Caucasus* (Gainesville: University Press of Florida, 1994).
11. Hadar, 'The Last Days of Likud,', p.67.
12. Warren Christopher, 'The Strategic Priorities of American Foreign Policy', *Dispatch* 4, No. 47 (1993), p.797.

13. For detailed information on the new trends in Turkish foreign policy, see Kemal Kirisci, 'New Patterns of Turkish Foreign Policy Behavior', in Cigdem Balim, *et al.* (eds), *Turkey: Political, Social and Economic Challenges in the 1990s* (Leiden: E.J. Brill, 1995).

14. For an Arab view that regards Israel as a potential threat to both Arabs and Iranians, see 'el-edau' el-mustriku li-Israil yekfi li-giyami tehalufi Arabiyyi-Iraniyyi' (Israeli activities are enough to provoke tensions between Arabs and Iranians), *al-Aalem*, 22 February 1997, p.27. For a Western perspective on the same discussion, see Moura Naim, 'L'attitude d'Israel et des Etats-Unis Suscite un Rapprochement entre les Pays Arabes et l'Iran' (The attitude of the US and Israel is leading to rapproachement between Iran and the Arab countries), *Le Monde*, 30–31 March 1997, p.2.

15. Hadar, 'The Last Days of Likud', p.68.

16. Anatoli Korinsky, 'Basbakan Ciller'in Basarili Ortadogu Gezisi Sona Erdi' (Prime Minister's Ciller's Succesful Middle East Trip Came to an End), *Moscow Radio*, 8 November 1994. Released by the Turkish General Directorate of Press.

17. DEIK (Dis Ekonomik Iliskiler Komisyonu/Turkish Foreign Economic Relations Board), *Turk ve Israilli Firmalar Arasinda Orta Asya Cumhuriyetlerinde Isbirligi Imkanlari Konulu Toplanti Notu* (Summary Notes of the conference on possible cooperation among Turkish–Israeli firms in the Central Asian republics), Istanbul, 10 December 1996.

18. Some Arab circles are willing to see Erbakan take sides with the anti-Israeli camp and they provide support to him bearing this position in mind. For further information, see 'el-mafyave'l ahzab el-Almaniyye tetehalefu li-muhavelati Iskati hukumet er-Refah' (Germany and Mafia behave contradictorily for the failure of the Refah government), *al-Mujtama'a*, 3 February 1997, p.38; 'Erbakan Yutalibu 'Israel' et-Tahalli an Tecavuzatiha' (Erbakan demanded Israeli withdrawal from occupied lands), *al-Aalem*, 19 April 1997, p.4.

19. For further information, see John M. Nomikos, *Looking Back to See Forwards: Israel–Turkey Defense Relations,* RIES Research Paper, No. 39 (July 1997).

20. Sami Kohen, 'Israil ile Stratejik Diyalog' (Strategic Dialogue with israel), *Milliyet*, 7 May 1997, p.5. For the historical background of Turkish–Israeli relations within the context of the Palestinian–Israeli peace process, see Bülent Aras, 'The Impact of the Palestinian–Israeli Peace Process on Turkish Foreign Policy', *Journal of South Asian and Middle Eastern Studies* 20, No. 2 (Winter 1997).

21. John Pomfret, 'Some Neighborly Advice-Turkey Strengthens Its Ties to Israel', *Washington Post, National Weekly Addition*, 10–16 June 1997, pp.16–17.

22. 'Alakatuna mea Israil Hedefuha Istikrar el-Mintika' (Target of our relations with Israel is to achieve peace in the region), *al-Wasat*, 23 June 1997, pp.16–17.

23. Adam Garfinkle, 'U.S.–Israeli Relations After the Cold War', *Orbis 40*, No. 4 (Autumn 1996), p.569; also see Bülent Aras, 'U.S.–Central Asian Relations: A View From Turkey', *MERIA Journal* 1, No. 1, (http://www.biu.ac.il/SOC/besa/meria/aras.html), 1996.

24. Turkish Ministry of Foreign Affairs, TICA *Eurasian File*, No. 20 (1994).

25. George E. Gruen, 'Dynamic Progress in Turkish–Israeli Relations', *Israel Affairs* 1, No. 4 (1995), p.66.

26. Robert O. Freedman, 'Israeli–Russian Relations Since the Collapse of the Soviet Union', *Middle East Journal* 49, No. 2 (Spring 1995), p.237.

27. Obsestvennoye Rosiakoye Televidinya, *Vremya News Bulletin*, 7 May 1997; *Rossiiskiye Vesti*, 21 February 1997; *Pravda*, 22 February 1997.

28. For a recent analysis of possible Russian foreign-policy shifts, see *Nezavisimaya Gazeta*, 8 February 1997. In addition, Russian foreign-policy makers seek alternative partners from the East like China and South Korea. See 'Vi Rassiya' (From Russia), *Dagestanskaya Pravda*, 27 March 1997 and *Pravda*, 10 May 1997.

29. Scott Parish, 'Israeli Prime Minister in Moscow', *OMRI Daily Digest* (http://www.omri.cz), 12 March 1997.

30. Sergei Arutiunov, Chairman of the Department of Caucasian Studies at the Moscow Institute of Ethnology and Antropology (personal correspondence).

31. Abdulkerim Uregen, Chairman of the Department of Political Science at the Qafqaz University of Baku (personal correspondence). He provided the data that the size of the Jewish community in Azerbaijan is about 38,000, 18,000 of whom live in the Kuba district. During the Lenin era, the Soviet Jewish population had been transferred east and settled in Transcaucasia.

In the late 1970s, the Jewish national movement attempted to increase ethnic conciousness among the Jewish community of Azerbaijan, but these attempts only led to the migration of a limited number of Jewish to Israel.

32. Ehteshami and Murphy, 'The Non-Arab Middle East', p.97.
33. Henri J. Barkey, 'Iran and Turkey', in Alvin Z. Rubinstein and Oles M. Smolansky (eds), *Regional Power Rivalries in the New Eurasia: Russia, Turkey and Iran* (Armonk: M.E. Sharpe, 1995), p.155.
34. *Azerbaycan Zaman* (Baku), 29 August 1996; *Azerbaycan Gazetesi* (Baku), 30 August 1996.
35. Jane Hunter. 'Israel and Turkey: Arms for Azerbaijan?', *Middle East International,* (23 October 1992), p.12.
36. 'Israeli Premier Visits Azerbaijan', *Turan Analytical Review*, Turan News Agency, No. 357, 1 September 1997 (root@turan.azerbaijan.su).
37. Sule Kut, 'Yeni Turk Cumhuriyetlerinin Dis Politikalari' (Foreign policies of the New Turkic Republics), in Busra Ersanii Behar (ed.), *Bagimsizligin llk Yillari* (First Years of Independence), (Ankara: Ministry of Culture Pub., 1994), pp.253–4.
38. *Philadelphia Inquirer*, 21 July 1997.
39. Ehteshami and Murphy, 'The Non-Arab Middle East', pp.99–100.
40. BBC, Summary of World Broadcast (hereafter SWB), 31 August 1995, SU/2396, F/7.
41. SWB, 5 September 1997, SU/2400, F/3.
42. SWB, 31 August 1995, SU/2396, F/7.
43. Lowell Bezanis, foreign-policy analyst at the Open Media Research Institute (personal correspondence).
44. SWB, 24 August 1996. SU/2699, F/6.
45. Turk Sanayici vc Isadamlari Beynelhalk Cemiyeti (International Society of Turkish Industrialists and Businessmen), *Isadamlari Icin Azerbaycan El Rehberi '96* (*Azerbaijan Handbook of Businessmen '96*) (Baku: Caglayan. 1996), p.28.
46. Rafael Husainov, 'Netanyahu/Azerbaijan', *Voice of America*, 29 August 1997, Correspondent Report No. 2-219147, via Habarlar-L, *Azerbaijan News Distribution List* (Habarlar-L-Request@USC.edu).
47. 'Netanyahu Shops For Oil During Azeri Stopover', Reuters, 29 August 1997.
48. Jay Bushinsky, 'PM Discusses Oil Pipeline in Baku', *Jerusalem Post,* 31 August 1997.
49. 'Iran Radio Slams Azerbaijan for Hosting Israeli PM', Reuters, 30 August 1997.
50. 'Armenian Foreign Minister: Turco-Israeli Cooperation Perilous for Region', IRNA, 10 September 1997.
51. *Turan*, in Russian, 12 January 1999, cited in FBIS-SOV-99-012, 13 January 1999.
52. *Al-Hawadith*, in Arabic, 18 December 1998, pp.16–19, cited in FBIS-LAT-99-009, 12 January 1999.
53. Robert O. Freedman, 'Israel and Central Asia: A Preliminary Analysis', *Central Asia Monitor*, No. 2 (1993), p.17. As Freedman argues, it is difficult to determine Iran's role in this attitude toward Israel.
54. *Al-Aalem,* 7 September 1993.
55. Carol R. Savietz, 'Central Asia: Emerging Relations with the Arab States and Israel', in Hafeez Malik (ed.), *Central Asia: Its Strategic Importance and Future Prospects* (New York: St Martin's Press, 1994), p.319.
56. *Christian Science Monitor*, 25 September 1992.
57. 'Dairy Cattle Husbandry Demonstration Project in Uzbekistan', via web page of Israeli Ministry of Foreign Affairs (http://www.israel-mfa.gov.il).
58. *Financial Times,* 6 May 1992.
59. Ehteshami and Murphy, 'The Non-Arab Middle East', p.101.
60. *Christian Science Monitor*, 25 September 1992.
61. 'Fact Sheets: Central Asian Republics', *Dispatch* 5, No. 19 (1994), p.294; *Askabat Aksami* (Askhabat), 7 February 1994; *Ahal Durmusu* (Askhabat), 21 July 1994.
62. *Turkmenistan* (Askhabat), 27 March 1996.
63. SWB, 13 March 1995, SU 2250, p. G/17; *Askabat Aksami*, 1 June 1995.
64. DEIK, *Turk ve Israil'li*, p.3.
65. Lowell Bezanis, 'Niyazov in Egypt, Israel', *OMRI Daily Digest* (http://www.omri.cz), 26 May 1995; *Turkmenistan,* 1 April 1995.

66. David Harris, 'Sharon, Russians to Discuss Gas Deal', *Jerusalem Post* (http://www.jposl.ci), 14 March 1997.
67. David Harris, 'Merhav Wins $500m. Refinery Upgrade Deal in Turkmenistan', *Jerusalem Post* (http://www.jpost corn), 26 August 1996; *Turkmenistan*, 8 October 1996.
68. Interview with Mehmet Tuma, Department of International Relations, Turkmenbashi University, Askhabat, 30 April 1997, Istanbul.
69. Ibid.
70. Gruen, 'Dynamic Progress', p.56.
71. *Financial Times,* 28 January 1993.
72. DEIK, *Turk ve Israil'li*, p.6.
73. SWB, 4 October 1995, SU 2425, G/5.
74. Ibid. Despite this statement, Kazakhstan also seeks to develop ties with Iran; see 'Velayeti fi-Kazakhstan li-Te'kit-it-Teavun' (Velayati is in Kazakhstan to consolidate cooperation), *Al-Aalem*, 26 April, 1997, p.4.
75. 'Fact Sheets', p.288.
76. Aluf Ben, 'A Change in Israeli–Iranian Relations', *Ha 'aretz,* 10 November 1996, quoted on the home page of the Foreign Ministry of Israel on the Internet. For the Iranian perspective on Turkish activities in the former Soviet South, see Firouzeh Nahavandi, 'Russia, Iran and Azerbaijan: The Historic Origins of Iranian Foreign Policy', in Bruno Coppietres (ed.), *Contested Borders in the Caucasus* (Brussels, VUB University Press, 1996).
77. For a likely argument, see Kemal Kirisci *et al.*, *Political and Economic Cooperation and Integration in the Middle East* (Istanbul: TESEV, 1997).
78. Any reversal in the peace process, however, has the potential to threaten the emergence of this peaceful Middle East environment. For information on the current state of the peace process, see Patrice Claude, 'Un Inquietant Silence est Tombe sur la Poudriere de Gaza' (A worrisome silence has fallen over the powderkeg of Gaza), *Le Monde*, 15 April 1997, p.4, and Alexandre Buccianti, 'La Ligue Arabe Reprend une Attitude Hostile a l'Etat Hebreu' (The Arab League is again taking a hostile attitude towards the Jewish state), *Le Monde*, April 2, 1997, p.2.
79. Ehteshami and Murphy, 'The Non-Arab Middle East', p.103.
80. Jay Bushinsky, 'Russia's Role', *Jerusalem Post* (http://www.jposi.com), 2 February 1997.
81. *Turkish Daily News*, 4 September 1997.
82. Lowell Bezanis, 'Turco-Israeli Accord Aggravates Regional Tensions', *OMRI Analytical Brief* (http://www.omri.cz), 18 April 1996.

5

US–CENTRAL ASIAN RELATIONS

The former US president Ronald Reagan told Notre Dame University students in May 1981, 'The West will not contain Communism, it will transcend Communism. We will not bother to denounce it, we'll dismiss it as a sad, bizarre chapter in human history whose last pages are even now being written.'[1] After nearly a decade, his edict became reality and the 'evil empire' collapsed together with its Marxist–Leninist ideology. The USSR's disintegration ended the Cold War era and is reshaping world politics.

One key development is the emergence of new republics in a Central Asia, which has become, in effect, the Middle East's northern frontier. The predominantly Turkish-speaking populations in these republics has increased Turkey's importance in the US government's eyes.[2] Turkey's strategy toward this region tries to mobilize its cultural, ethnic and linguistic ties to the Turkic republics.

This study's purpose is to analyze US relations with the Central Asian Republics of Kazakhstan, Uzbekistan, Kirgyzstan, Turkmenistan and Tajikistan. It will also evaluate Turkey's view of this situation and the relation of the new states – and issues raised – with Middle East politics.

POLITICAL RELATIONS

In this area, the main US goals are to increase stability, speed up democratization, introduce a free-market economy and make sure that it operates smoothly, increase commercial activity, control nuclear weapons and encourage human-rights standards. The principal priority can be defined as blocking the spread of influence of existing radical regimes and preventing the creation of new ones.[3] US policy wants to see the Central Asian Republics succeed so they will not be replaced by anti-Western radical regimes that may threaten international peace and security.

While US policy-makers generally share these goals, they differ over how much US involvement is needed. Those supporting an active policy warn that instability here could damage Middle East states having good relations with Washington, and especially Turkey.[4]

Moreover, this view emphasizes the existence of nuclear weapons and equipment for producing them in this region as posing a danger of proliferation to radical Third World states or terrorist organizations. Limiting Russian and Iranian influence in the area is another important consideration. Thus, the United States would be well advised to increase support for the region and build strong bilateral relations.[5] Those favoring intervention also want to gain commercial advantages over China, South Korea and European states in penetrating the Central Asian market.[6]

Those criticizing America's current policy and seeking less involvement in Central Asia say the region does not mean much for US interests and that Turkey and other friendly states can preserve stability, avoiding a radical Islamic threat in this part of the Middle East. Efforts to promote democracy, they argue, could lead to instability or authoritarianism. The oil and markets of these new states are deemed too unimportant, at least in the present, to justify US activism there.[7]

Of these two approaches, the first has been dominant so far, particularly in the second Clinton term. The United States quickly recognized the newly independent republics following the USSR's collapse in 1991 and, as the Deputy Secretary of State Strobe Talbott noted, evaluated each nation's characteristics in building different types of links.[8] This can be seen in a country-by-country survey.

The key legislation for dealing with these countries is a law entitled Freedom for Russia and Emerging Eurasian Democracies and Open Markets (FREEDOM), passed in 1992 and providing for special aid.[9] The United States has a vital interest in encouraging the economic growth that would secure the sovereignty of the Central Asian states. It goes almost without saying that, without broad-based economic development, the Central Asian states will remain hostage to political instability. The competitive advantage of American companies in infrastructure development promises much of contributing significantly to regional economic growth.

The US government recognized Kazakhstan first of all on 25 December 1991. There were an impressive number of high-level visits between the two states. Kazakhstan's President Nursultan Nazarbayev went to Washington, on 18–20 May 1992. Vice President Al Gore reciprocated in September 1993, followed by Secretary of State Warren Christopher in October 1994.[10] During Nazarbayev's second trip to the United States, he and Clinton signed a Democratic Cooperation Agreement emphasizing democratic values, human rights and the rule of law.[11] In April 1995, the US Defense Secretary William Perry traveled to Kazakhstan.[12]

US–Kirgyzstan relations followed a similar pattern. Washington recognized Kirgyzstan on 25 December 1991 and opened an embassy in Bishkek in

February 1992. The Kirgyz President, Asker Akayev, visited the United States, on 15–22 May 1993, meeting Clinton, Gore and Christopher. An aid agreement was signed and Gore went to Kirgyzstan in December 1993, signing an accord to facilitate investments and for a joint agricultural project.

Despite ups and downs, these two are ahead of others in the democratization process, according to reports prepared by American think tanks.[13] In relations with these and other Central Asian states, Washington has taken a series of initiatives to promote a transition to democracy, including exchange and educational programs in diplomacy, education, journalism and elections.[14]

US relations with Turkmenistan and Uzbekistan, however, are at a slightly lower level, since these two have made less progress toward democracy and a free-market economy.[15] Relations have been more strained with Uzbekistan over its record regarding civil liberties and human rights. Nonetheless, Perry emphasized Uzbekistan's strategic importance during his April 1995 visit there and reiterated US support for its stability.[16]

Tajikistan is the country with which the US administration has had the lowest level of relations, despite recognizing that country as early as 25 December 1991 and opening an embassy in Dushanbe in March 1992. The main reason has been a civil war and instability continuing to the present. The United States has held talks about sending humanitarian aid to Tajikistan and State Department officials have participated in peace talks between the warring parties in there as observers within the UN.

OTHER POWERS AND THEIR IMPACT ON US STRATEGY

A half-dozen other states, each with its own interests and assets, also play a role in the Middle East's northern frontier. US policy must take these factors into consideration. Some of them reinforce American goals, others pose threats – or potential dangers – to US interests.

Clearly, Russia continues to be the most important among the regional powers. Until 1993, it pursued a Western-oriented policy but then revised this stand because of Western attempts to expand NATO's eastern border and since it received less aid than expected from the West.[17] Russia has restructured the Commonwealth of Independent States (CIS) to tighten cooperation, sought to improve economic and political links to China, and improved relations with radical Middle East states, especially Iran and Iraq.[18] Russia's growing dialogue with Iran, Iraq and even Libya clashes with US policy. Such differences might be reflected in Central Asia as well.

The People's Republic of China can also play an important role in the region.[19] China's *rapprochement* with Russia enhances their overlapping interests in Central Asia and thus they may cooperate.[20] Many American analysts view China as a principal great power in the forthcoming century. The way a US–Russia–China triangle works in the coming years will have a big effect on the area's countries.

In addition, several states friendly to the United States – Turkey, Israel and European countries – have rapidly developed political and economic relations with the Central Asian republics. Despite commercial rivalries, a common opposition to radical Islamic forces and support for stability and a free-market economy, makes these nations' political-economic penetration of the region a positive factor for US policy.

The Russian standpoint, however, may be different, especially given Moscow's concern over the European Union's growing economic and political integration with its former sphere of influence in Eastern European. European as well as American activity in Central Asia may be seen by Russia as a threat close to its own southern border.[21]

From Turkey's perspective, the appearance of five new states in Central Asia has caused a radical foreign-policy shift and a search for ways to gain influence in these republics.[22] Turkey does not, however, go to the region with chauvinist (i.e. pan-Turkic) aims. While the Central Asian states look to Turkey as a successful example, Ankara wants to spread its own model of secularism in an Islamic society, parliamentary democracy, and a free-market economy.[23] It appears that US cooperation with Turkey regarding Central Asia will continue in the coming years.

Another country with a desire to play a key role in the region is Israel.[24] It seeks to find friends in the Middle East, profitable markets and forces opposing the spread of radical Islamic revolutionary movements. Within this framework, Israel and Turkey cooperate regarding Central Asia, especially seeking to block Iran's power in the area.

In summary, post-Cold War balances have brought the United States, Turkey, Israel and Europe under the same umbrella of interest and general aims. It should be remembered, of course, that these states do not have identical goals and priorities, especially regarding commercial rivalry.

While Russia is the area's most important power, the above-mentioned states' concern is mostly focused on Iran. The formation of new countries, whose citizens are mostly Muslims, at the Middle East's northern edge gives Iran a unique opportunity to shed its international isolation. Given the power vacuum following the USSR's collapse, this is exactly what the Western world – and especially the United States – fears.

Iran has made serious initiatives toward these states, using its geographic advantage by offering them free passage through its own territory and by providing an alternative model to governments and opposition groups.[25] Iran knows it lacks the financing Central Asia needs. Consequently, Iran requires a 'big partner'. Russia is one possibility for this role; India also represents an interesting alternative.[26] Russia's choice of whether to work with or against Iran is going to be a critical factor in the regional power equation.

ECONOMIC RELATIONS

Aid and Cooperation

The first goal of US aid to the newly independent states is encouragement of the private sector. In FY 1995, Washington set aside $23 million for this purpose plus $10.5 million for Kazakhstan, Kirgyzstan and Uzbekistan to engage in economic restructuring. Technical aid and training programs to support a free-market economy and develop the private sector focus on such ventures as agriculture, small- and medium-scale enterprise, communications and banking.[27] Countries ready to carry out reforms have priority in receiving these funds. Table 1 shows the total aid given to the Central Asian republics in 1996 and the planned total to be given in 1997.

TABLE 5.1
1996 AND 1997 FISCAL YEARS (FY) AID PROGRAM ($ MILLION)

COUNTRY	1996 FY (estimated)	1997 FY (projected)
Kazakhstan	29.9	39
Uzbekistan	18.1	20
Kirgyzstan	17.6	20
Tajikistan	3.5	5
Turkmenistan	3.3	5
TOTAL	**72.4**	**89**

Source: Jim Nichol, *Central Asia's New States: Political Developments and Implications for US Interests*, CRS Issue Brief, (Washington: Library of Congress, 1996), p. 16.

Kazakhstan has been the main recipient of US aid, largely within the framework of Operation Provide Hope (OPH) or Department of Agriculture food programs.[28] All in all, official and private US institutions gave $24.3 million within the framework of OPH in 1992. Two years, later the United States provided $30 million in food aid alone.[29] There were also many unofficial programs. For example, a joint US–Japan health project vaccinated 500,000 infants against infectious diseases and gave $900,000 in medical equipment.

In FY 1994, the US Department of Agriculture gave $10 million to Turkmenistan for buying agricultural goods. Uzbekistan received $500,000 in food and $5.5 million in medical assistance under OPH. Nongovernmental groups gave $4.8 million more in medical aid.[30] The country most in need of humanitarian aid is Tajikistan. Humanitarian aid for Tajik immigrants in particular appeared in the FY 1994, 1995, 1996 US government budgets. This included $7.1 million in 1995 and $5 million for 1996. The United States also responded to a February 1996 UN Food and Agricultural Organization report calling for emergency aid to Tajikistan.[31] While the amounts of aid given are small compared with those received by other countries, they have a dispro-portionately large effect on these small, poor states.

Investment and Commerce

At the 1994 US–Central Asia Business Conference, the US Deputy Secretary of State, Strobe Talbott, said: 'The American businessmen are investing in the region because it is an attractive business, not because of altruism.' A Central Asia–America Initiative Fund was established there with a five-year budget of over $150 million.[32] Other agreements aimed to build the legal and material infrastructure needed to support such commercial efforts, including the Kazakh military industries.

The US Eximbank provided short-term funds and guarantees to Turkmenistan and Uzbekistan necessary for purchasing food and medical equipment. Furthermore, the US Overseas Private Investment Corporation (OPIC) signed separate agreements with five Central Asian states.[33]

In February 1993, the US administration signed an agreement with Kazakhstan granting it most-favored-nation status. The parties opened com-mercial offices and worked to improve bilateral economic relations. In May 1992 another agreement gave American entrepreneurs special privileges and it was strengthened in October 1993 with a protocol abolishing double taxa-tion. In addition, within the agreement's framework, OPIC provided $80 million dollars' financing to two companies exploring for oil in Kazakhstan.

Economic relations with Kirgyzstan followed a similar course, with a most-favored-nation agreement (August 1992) followed by an investment agreement four months later. Similar agreements were signed with Uzbekistan in November 1993 and March 1944. Less emphasis was put on Turkmenistan and Tajikistan, though several mutual investment agreements were also signed with them.[34]

Data on foreign trade and trade relations (Table 5.2) reflect the dimensions of the developing commercial relations, with oil being the main component.

TABLE 5.2
US ANNUAL TRADE WITH THE CENTRAL ASIAN REPUBLICS ($1,000,000)

COUNTRY	EXPORTS 92/93/94	IMPORTS 92/93/94	TRADE BALANCE 92/93/94
Kazakhstan	15/68/131	21/41/60	-6/27/71
Uzbekistan	51/73/90	a/7/3	51/66/87
Kirgyzstan	2/18/6	1/2/8	1/16/-2
Tajikistan	9/12/15	2/18/60	7/-6/-44
Turkmenistan	35/46/13	71/2/23	4/44/136
Total	**112/217/309**	**31/70/154**	**77/147/248**

a: Less than 500 thousands $.

Source: US Department of Commerce, *Statistical Abstract of the United States 1995* (Springfield: National Technical Information Service, 1995).

In that respect, Russia's growing assertiveness in the Central Asian Republics would damage US economic interests by preventing American firms' access to those economies. Big companies such as Chevron and Philip Morris have invested about $3 billion in the region and are expected to put in several times more in the coming years. A major agreement has been signed between the US oil company Chevron and Kazakhstan to extract oil in Kazakhstan's Tengiz and Korolev regions, with a 40-year duration and an investment of up to $20 billion.[35] There are also US–Israel, US–Turkey, or US–Turkey–Israel joint projects.[36]

SECURITY RELATIONS

One of Washington's main security problems in Central Asia is the disarmament of the nuclear weapons in Kazakhistan and the regulation of activities regarding the production of nuclear arms in the region. There have been voices in Kazakhstan public opinion advocating that the country remain a 'nuclear power' by holding onto weapons left there by the USSR. Still, Almaty ratified the Strategic Arms Reduction Treaty and the Lisbon protocol on 22 May 1992 to give up these arms. This status was confirmed by a US–Russia–Ukraine agreement 1994 and the 28 March 1994 Yeltsin–Nazarbayev accord.[37] By April 1995, 1,040 SS-18 missile warheads were transferred to Russia.[38] US aid to Kazakhstan is in exchange for safely transferring the weapons.

America's security concerns comprise not only nuclear weapons but also nuclear research and the power reactors in Uzbekistan. There is much concern that nuclear weapons might be sold to radical Third World countries and terrorist groups. There are reports that the CIA and Mossad keep the region's nuclear technology experts under watch.[39]

America's other security concern is radical Islam in the region, especially as a force whose spread would be accelerated by victories in Central Asia. This may be less likely than it appears, given the actual political culture in Central Asia and the importance of ethnic nationalism. In addition, the diffusion of Sufism as the main dynamic form taken by Islam is not conducive to revolutionary ideology.[40]

The first movement that made the West uneasy about Central Asia occurred in 1988, when Uzbek students used Islamic terms as slogans during a sudden demonstration in Taskhent.[41] After this demonstration, new developments regarding Islam in the other Central Asian states have been evaluated in American political and academic circles as the diffusion of radical Islam to various degrees.[42]

The Islamic Republic of Iran stands at the point at which the spread of nuclear weapons and anxiety concerning radical Islam intersect. One of

America's most important security targets is to contain Iran and prevent it from exporting its regime to the region. Iran's establishment of good relations not only with the Shiite population but with other communities in the region as well has drawn America's attention. A nuclear-reactor project between Russia and Iran also deepened US concerns.[43]

At the moment it seems that no detailed studies have been conducted on differences between the Islamic revivalism of Iran and the basic dynamics of Central Asian Islam, and whether one could directly feed the other. Moreover, the factor of Iran's national interests (including an unspoken but implicit Persian nationalism) to widen Tehran's influence in the area may compete with and undercut any desire to spread revolution or revolutionary Islamic ideology.

America's third security concern in Central Asia is civil wars and potential border conflicts. In places where there is instability, as in Tajikistan, the situation obstructs the development of democracy and the free-market economy that the United States strongly advocates. While the Clinton administration has argued these problems should be solved through the UN, it does not appear sympathetic to the idea Nazarbayev suggested in 1994 to establish a regional peace force and give it the status of a UN peacekeeping force.[44] As the only remaining superpower, the United States has been asked to bring the warring factions to the negotiating table for mediation, and suggest appropriate principles for equitable settlements. The United States should respond to such requests with support for further peacekeeping and monitoring efforts.

Finally, US policy is concerned with the safety of oil and gas pipelines in the region and ensuring free access to the oilfields there. The most important pipeline route in Central Asia would transport oil from the giant Tengiz oilfield in Kazakhstan, developed by the US-based Chevron corporation, toward Europe and the Mediterranean. According to a specialist, 'The US should support a pipeline route through the territory of Georgia and Turkey that will bring oil from Eurasia to a Mediterranean port such as Ceyhan in Turkey.'[45] It is clear that Turkey is again an important ally in this regard.

As Ariel Cohen argued, 'Lobbying is under way in Washington to allow pipelines to run south from Central Asia through Iran. Such an oil route might make sense economically, but it would give transit tariff revenues to Iran's militant regime and tie US oil to Persian Gulf terminals, further undermining the security of the oil supply.'[46] Ankara had resorted to the American pressure lobbies to influence the options and decisions of the international oil consortium, which is managed by Western companies and has the task of exploiting Baku's oil reserves.

CONCLUDING OBSERVATIONS

In the early 1990s the end of the half-century-long Cold War era gave the

United States more power and freedom of maneuver than ever before. An important outcome of the USSR's collapse has been the opening of new horizons for the ex-Soviet republics. Washington has undertaken initiatives for the healthy integration of these states into the world system. In Central Asia, US policy tries to maximize long-range strategic aims by building relations to the different countries.

From Turkey's perspective, the US dimension is also an important consideration in formulating policy toward an area where Turkey has strategic, economic, and ethnic/cultural interests. Former Prime Minister Tansu Çiller's announcement to the West that Turkey now leads 200 million Turkic speakers and not just its own 60 million people shows how activity in this region is seen as enhancing Turkey's importance. At the same time, Turkey worries – perhaps excessively – about the possibility of a US–Russia entente to have hegemony over Central Asia.

In the post-Soviet era, relations with the Russian Federation have gained more importance for Turkey compared with the Cold War period. On the one hand, it is contrary to Turkey's interests if there is a new line of division in Europe. But on the other hand, if the West gives Russia a free hand regarding the former USSR republics (which Russians call the 'near abroad') that is also a matter for Turkey's concern.

Thus, the future of Russian and Iranian influence in Central Asia raises important questions for both the United States and Turkey, albeit in somewhat different ways. The extent to which Central Asia becomes part of the Middle East will also be an interesting development which may draw the involvement of regional powers and affect the area's balance of power.

NOTES

1. Peter Schweizer, 'Who Broke the Evil Empire?' *National Review* 46, No. 10 (30/5/1994) p. 47.
2. Interview with Graham Fuller, a senior specialist in International Relations in RAND Corporation, Istanbul, 4 October 1996.
3. 'Statement before the Subcommittee on Foreign Operations, Export Financing and Related Programs of the House Appropriations Committee, Washington, DC, May 10, 1994' (1994): *Dispatch* 5, No. 21 (23 May 1994): pp. 332–8.
4. Warren Christopher, 'Toward a Secure, Free, and Fully Integrated Europe', *Dispatch* 5, No. 25 (20 June 1994), p. 403.
5. Ibid.
6. Strobe Talbott, 'An Address by US Deputy Secretary at the US Central Asia Business Conference Washington, DC, USA, May 3, 1994', *Presidents & Prime Ministers* 3, No. 5 (September/October 1994), p. 281.
7. Jim Nichol, *Central Asia's New States: Political Developments and Implications for US Interests* (CRS Issue Brief. Washington: Library of Congress, 1996), p. 16.
8. Strobe Talbott, 'Promoting Democracy and Prosperity in Central Asia', *Dispatch* 5, No. 19 (5 September 1994), p. 34.
9. 'Statement by White House Press Secretary Dee Dee Myers, Washington, DC, 15 July 1994', *Dispatch* 5, No. 30 (25 July 1994), p. 510.
10. *Turkish Daily News*, 11 December 1993.

11. Ibid., 16 February 1994.
12. Ibid., 6 April 1995.
13. *Human Rights and Democratization in the Newly Independent States of the Former Soviet Union* (CSCE Report. Washington, DC: GPO, 1993)
14. 'Fact Sheets: Central Asian Republics', *Dispatch* 5, (9 May 1994), p. 282.
15. Christopher Panico, 'Turkmenistan Unaffected by Winds of Democratic Change', *RFE/RL Research Report*, (22 January 1993), pp. 6–10; Esedullah Oguz, 'Dunden Bugune Turkmenistan' (Turkmenistan From Past to Today), *Yeni Forum* 17, No. 325 (June 1995), pp. 41–7; Esedullah Oguz, 'Turkmenistan'da Basin ve Yayin Ozgurlugu' (Freedom of Press and Media in Turkmenistan), *Yeni Forum* 16, No. 317 (October 1996), pp. 23–8.
16. Jim Nichol, *Central Asia's New States: Political Developments and Implications for US Interests* (CRS Issue Brief. Washington: Library of Congress, 1996), p. 3.
17. Stanislav Lunev, 'Future Changes in Russian Military Policy', *Prism: A Bi-Weekly on the Post-Soviet States* 2, No. 3 (February 1996).
18. Peter Ferdinand, 'The New Central Asia and China', in Peter Ferdinand (ed.), *The New Central Asia and Its Neighbours* (London, 1994), pp. 8–11.
19. Chen Mingshan and He Xiquan, 'Features and Prospects of the Situation in the Central Asian Region', *Foreign Affairs Journal* (Beijing), No. 37 (1995); Chang Qing, 'Brief Analysis on China's Relations with the Five Central Asian Nations', *Foreign Affairs Journal* (Beijing), No. 33 (1994).
20. Olgan Bekar, 'Cin ve Bati Turkistan' (China and Western Turkestan), *Avrasya Dosyasi* 2, No. 2 (Summer 1995), pp. 47–55; Bülent Aras, 'Cin–Orta Asya Iliskileri' (Chinese–Central Asian Relations), *Yeni Forum* 17, No. 326 (July 1996), pp. 15–16.
21. Sharly Cross, 'The Questions of NATO Expansion: Searching for the Optimal Solution', *Mediterranean Quarterly* 7, No. 1 (Winter 1996); Stanley R Sloan, 'US Perspectives on NATO's Future', *International Affairs* 71, No. 2 (1995).
22. Kemal Kirisci, 'New Patterns of Turkish Foreign Policy Behavior', in Cigdem Balim et al. (eds) *Turkey: Political, Social and Economic Challanges in the 1990s* (Leiden: E.J. Brill, 1995).
23. Bahri Yilmaz, 'Turkey After the Dissolution of the Soviet Union', *Balkan Forum* (Skopje) 2, (Spring 1994), p. 194.
24. Bülent Aras, 'Iran'in Degisen Guvenlik Dengesi Cercevesinde Orta Asya ve Kafkasya Cumhuriyetleri ile Iliskileri' (The Relations between Iran and the Caucasian and Central Asian Republics), *Avrasya Dosyasi* 3, No. 3 (Autumn 1996).
25. Ibid.
26. P. Stobdan, 'Emergence of Central Asia: Strategic Implications', *Strategic Analysis* (New Delhi) 18, No. 3 (June 1995).
27. Nichol, *Central Asia's New States*.
28. 'Statement before the Subcommittee', pp. 335–6.
29. Fact Sheets, 290.
30. Ibid., 293–8.
31. Nichol, *Central Asia's New States*, p. 14.
32. Talbott, 'Promoting Democracy', pp. 280–2.
33. Nichol, *Central Asia's New States*, p. 14.
34 'The US and Kazakhstan: A Strategic Economic and Political Relationship', *Dispatch* 5, No. 8 (21 February 1994), pp. 97–9.
35. *Milliyet*, 8 April 1993; *Dunya*, 7 April 1993.
36. Ibid., 11 November 1994.
37. Zachary S. Davis, and Jason D. Ellis, *Nuclear Proliferation: Problems in the States of the Former Soviet Union* (CRS Issue Brief, Washington: Library of Congress, 1995).
38. Amy F. Woolf and Theodor W. Galdi, *Nuclear Weapons in the Former Soviet Union: Location, Command, and Control* (CRS Issue Brief, Washington: Library of Congress, 1996).
39. Anoushiravan Ehteshami and Emma C. Murphy, 'The Non-Arab Middle East States and the Caucassian/Central Asian States: Iran and Israel', *International Relations* (London) 12, No. 1 (April 1994).
40. Mehrdad Haghayeghi, 'Islam and Politics in Central Asia', *World Affairs* 156, No. 4 (Spring 1994), pp. 186–9.
41. Martha B. Olcott, 'Gorbachev's National Dilemma', *Journal of International Affairs*, No. 42 (Spring 1989).

42. Mutahir Ahmet, 'Radikal Islam ve Orta Asya' (Radical Islam and Central Asia), *Avrasya Etütleri*, No. 3 (Autumn 1994), pp. 55–61; Robert D. Kangas, 'Ozbekistan'da Islam'in Uc Yuzu' (Three Faces of Islam in Uzbekistan), *Yeni Forum* 17, No. 323 (April 1996), pp. 19–23; Abdujabar Abduvakhitov, 'Islamic Revivalism Uzbekistan', in Dale Eickelman (ed.), *Russia's Muslim Frontiers* (Bloomington: Indiana University Press, 1993), pp. 96–7.
43. *Milliyet*, 6 May 1995.
44. Nichol, *Central Asia's New States*, p. 6.
45. Ariel Cohen, 'Yeni Buyuk Oyun: Avrasya'da Boru Hatti Siyaseti' (New Great Game and Pipeline Politics in Eurasia), *Avrasya Etudleri* 3, No. 1 (Spring 1996), p. 16.
46. Ariel Cohen, 'US Policy in the Caucasus and Central Asia: Building a New "Silk Road" to Economic Prosperity', Backgrounder, No. 1132 (July 1997), http://www.heritage.org/library/categories/forpol/bg1132.html.

6

THE RELATIONS BETWEEN EUROPE AND THE TURKIC REPUBLICS

The collapse of the Soviet Union and the dissolution of the Eastern bloc has dramatically affected the countries of Europe. Addressing these historic and profound events has been a dialectical process – just as European nations have been affected, they have also contributed to developments in the formerly Soviet-controlled sphere. The foundation for Europe's present actions grew out of efforts at political and economic integration in the mid-1980s. These initiatives toward lull integration were highly popular and economically successful, creating a psychological effect in the Eastern bloc that contributed to the transformation in those countries. It is a widely accepted proposition that this spillover effect played a part in the collapse of the Soviet system.[1] Meanwhile, the dissolution of the Warsaw Pact has positively affected Europe's economic integration process, as it has allowed a shift in focus away from traditional security problems. Accordingly, European countries have accelerated their political and economic cooperation and the European Community has been transformed into the European Union (EU). The collapse of the Cold War system has also created new economic opportunities in the East for European countries.

One of the countries most affected by these recent developments has been Turkey. Turkey's government decided to become a part of the Western camp just after World War Two, and, although it has experienced difficult periods in its relations with the West, it has nonetheless maintained its undeniable importance for the European countries. Turkey was caught unprepared when the Soviet Union collapsed but soon succeeded in establishing significant relations with the emerging Turkic republics,[2] particularly through the efforts of nongovernmental organizations. As a result, Turkey is poised to play a vital role in future relations between Europe and these republics.

In this study, the relations of European countries with the Turkic Republics and Turkey's position in respect to both are examined against the background of the international dynamic described above. First, the regional profile of the EU and its relations within the framework of its aid plan to the former Soviet republics are investigated. Second, because individual national economies figure prominently in negotiations, relations between individual European countries and the Turkic republics are analyzed, with an emphasis on economic ventures in these republics. Third, the prospects for the success of continued economic and political relations are discussed, with special attention given to the role of Turkey as a facilitator in these relations. Finally, I suggest that Turkey is of crucial importance to European efforts to develop sustainable economic and political ties with the Turkic republics. Moreover, the position of Turkey in relation to the Turkic republics should help it in its efforts to join the EU. Turkey can best serve a facilitating role if it is made a member of the EU – a development that would have positive political, economic and security implications for the entire region.

EUROPE'S INTERESTS IN THE TURKIC REPUBLICS

After the dissolution of the Soviet Union, the former Soviet republics gained the status of legitimate successors to the Soviet Union following a session of foreign ministers of the Conference on Security and Cooperation in Europe (CSCE) in January 1992. After this recognition, Azerbaijan, Kazakhstan, Kirgyzstan, Turkmenistan and Uzbekistan were accepted as full members of the CSCE.[3]

The primary impetus for the recognition of these countries was to pre-empt a possible wave of instability originating from the former Soviet republics. It was feared that this instability could spread throughout Europe because the reciprocal deterrence system of NATO versus the Warsaw Pact no longer existed. Part of the concern, which continues to this day, was that radical religious movements might gain governmental control in these still-forming republics. The fear of Islamic fundamentalism is voiced by American think tanks and is also taken seriously by European governments.[4] At the same time, European countries have also recognized the potential for tremendous economic benefits in increased relations with the Turkic republics. As a result of these dual interests, the nations of Europe have attempted to develop links with the Turkic republics on various levels. On the political level, the goals of the EU have included global recognition of each republic and influence on structural transformations in these countries, as discussed in the subsection on EU aid and cooperation. On another level, Europe's goal has been the facilitation of economic activities by European nationals in these republics, as described in subsection on economic relations.

EU Aid and Cooperation with the Turkic Republics

The European Union has been extending aid programs (called TACIS – Technical Assistance for the Commonwealth of Independent States) to the 12 former Soviet republics since 1991, and to Mongolia since 1994. These aid programs consist of technical assistance, food, credits, low-priced agricultural products and medicine. The main goals of TACIS are to strengthen democracy in these countries and to support their economies during the transition to a market economy. As discussed below, partnership agreements with Kazakhstan and Kirgyzstan were signed in 1995 according to these principles. Negotiations for agreements with other countries continue.[5]

The specific areas of priority for TACIS include: reconstruction of state services; development of the private sector in agriculture, infrastructure, energy, telecommunications and transportation; nuclear security; environmental reforms; and reforms in public services and education. Much has been accomplished, particularly in the development of statistical data, which are indispensable for modern democracies and market economics. The largest proportion of TACIS funding goes to Ukraine and Russia. Among the Turkic republics, Kazakhstan receives the largest portion. (See Tables 6.1 and 6.2.)

Economic Relations Between Europe and the Turkic Republics

In the coming years, the level of economic ties will be the most important factor in determining the state of relations between the EU and the Turkic republics. The European states, aware of the verities of *realpolitik,* know that they cannot establish secure relations by cooperation agreements and promises alone. As a result, economic activity by European countries in the Turkic republics has gradually increased in recent years. This part of the study aims to analyze economic relations between the Turkic republics and European countries as a whole, according to the data available, with some reference to political developments as well.

Kazakhstan

Relations between Kazakhstan and the EU reached their most significant point to date in January 1995 with the signing of a ten-year agreement focusing primarily on economic cooperation, but which will also increase political, scientific, technological and cultural relations.[6] The Kazakh delegation was

TABLE 6.1
TACIS FUND: 1991–94 (million ECUs)

Year	Amount
1991	400
1992	450
1993	510
1994	510
TOTAL	**1,870**

Source: European Commission, TACIS Information Office, *What is TACIS?* 4 (1995).

TABLE 6.2
TACIS BUDGET: 1991–93 (million ECUs)

Country	Amount	Country	Amount
Russia	496.5	Georgia	12.7
Ukraine	119.2	Azerbaijan	12.5
Kazakhstan	40.4	Moldova	10.0
Belorussia	31.8	Turkmenistan	9.8
Armenia	20.8	Tajikistan	0.5
Uzbekistan	20.2	Multi-Country Projects	395
Kirgyzstan	19.6	Others	156
Baltic Countries	15.0	**TOTAL**	**1,360**

Source: European Commission, TACIS Information Office, *What is TACIS?* 4 (1995).

headed by President Nursultan Nazarbayev. The president of the EU's delegation was the French Foreign Minister Alain Juppe, who was then Council President of the EU. Jacques Santer, head of the European Commission, also took part in the official ceremony in Brussels.[7] Looking at the historic nature of this agreement, it is amazing that so much has evolved in relations in the short time following the collapse of the Soviet Union.

In December 1993, the government of Kazakhstan signed an agreement with seven Western oil companies in Almaty for the exploration of oil and gas reserves in the northern Caspian Sea.[8] This will lead to the lion's share of Kazakh oil going directly to European countries or being handled by their companies. According to British Petroleum's representative in Kazakhstan, the Caspian Sea contains one of the richest oilfields in the world.[9] Explorations of this vast oilfield, with an estimated reserve of 60 to 100 billion barrels of crude oil and $1.5 trillion worth of gas, will cost the Western countries more than $300 million. The agreement provides that this research will be completed within three years.[10] Ultimately, $20 billion in short-term and $60 billion in long-term commercial activity is expected as a result of this agreement.

The signing of the oil-exploration agreement is just one example of Kazakhstan's strengthening economic relations with European countries. In 1994, Prime Minister Sergei Tereschenko received a credit of $114 million from the European Bank of Research and Development.[11] A consortium led by a British company won a 'tender and license' to mine Vasilkovskoye, Kazakhstan's largest known gold deposit, estimated to contain 400 tons of gold.[12]

On 2 March 1995, another agreement was signed with primarily European oil companies for the rights to gas and oil reserves in the Karachanak region, further demonstrating the continuation of good relations. A source of friction arose when Kazakhstan's 1995 Parliamentary elections were declared illegal, which caused short-term anxiety that agreements signed with foreign oil companies would be annulled.[13] However, these fears were soon allayed when the agreements were recognized by governmental decree and relations returned to normal.

Kazakhstan's high level of trade with European countries is another indicator of its evolving relations with Europe.[14] Among EU members, Germany has the highest level of trade with Kazahstan, followed by Switzerland, England and Sweden, respectively.[15] (See Table 6.3.) Kazakhstan's imports from Europe consist primarily of machinery, transportation products, manufactured goods and chemicals. Its exports to Europe are made up of iron, steel and other raw metals.

TABLE 6.3
SHARES OF EUROPEAN COUNTRIES IN THE FOREIGN TRADE OF
KAZAKHSTAN IN 1998 ($ m)

Country	Exports	Imports
Germany	214.5	263.0
England	432.2	134.3
Italy	59.7	59.7
TOTAL EU	**701.4**	**1,410.6**

Source: Economist Intelligence Unit (EIU). Country profiles, Kazakhstan, Kirgyz Republic, Tajikistan, Turkmenistan, Uzbekistan (1999).

An unmistakably important factor influencing the high level of trade between Kazakhstan and Germany is the 900,000 Kazakh citizens of German descent. This has strongly affected Germany's attitude toward Kazakhstan, and this issue was a top priority in discussions between the foreign ministers of the two countries during Nazarbayev's visit to Bonn in March 1992. Germany recognizes the importance of this issue by providing aid to the regions where Kazakhs of German descent live, which increases the standard of living in these regions, and at the same time helps prevent the emigration of these people to Germany.[16] In 1996, the German government earmarked DM100 million to Kazakhstan from a total exportation credit of DM2.3 billion for Russia and other countries of the Commonwealth of Independent States.[17]

Azerbaijan

There was a period of rapid development in relations between Azerbaijan and Europe following Azerbaijan's independence. *Rapprochement* with the West and establishing relations with the European countries formed an important component of Azerbaijan's foreign-policy goals, revolving around its efforts to gain political support in its war against Armenia in the Nagorno-Karabakh region.[18] President Haydar Aliyev's official visit to France on 23 December 1993 presents one example of this effort. President François Mitterrand, who had recently signed both 'The Paris Article' within the framework of the CSCE and an agreement on friendship and cooperation, discussed relations between the two countries and promised that their ties would gain new vigor.[19] One of the most important outcomes of Aliyev's visit was Mitterrand's later warning to Armenian leaders concerning their attacks against Azerbaijan.

Aliyev also attended meetings with French business leaders and stressed that Azerbajian's goals of a transnational pipeline and other economic ventures were of secondary importance. He indicated that those countries that supported Azerbaijan's policies would receive his support in oil ventures and other economic activities.[20] In February 1994 Aliyev continued his efforts to increase relations with EU countries during his trip to London. This four-day visit consisted of meetings with Prime Minister John Major and British business leaders, and talks with oil company executives concerning the rich oil reserves in the Caucasus.[21]

Azerbaijan's relations with Germany have also steadily improved. Michael Schmunk, *chargé d'affaires* of Germany to the Azeri capital Baku, strongly emphasized the desire of German business owners to set up power stations, pipeline factories, breweries and factories to produce food and chemicals, and to undertake the restoration of existing abandoned factories.[22] The Foreign Minister, Klaus Kinkel, paid an official visit to Azerbaijan in December 1995, during which an agreement on cultural and economic cooperation between the two countries and a protocol stipulating that German business investments would be increased were signed.[23] The Azeri President's visit to Germany in June 1996 was a further indicator of the two countries' intentions to continue improving relations. Aliyev made clear statements expressing his interest in continuing to strengthen economic ties between the countries.[24] He also noted Germany's interest in the Caucasus, particularly in its efforts to bring about a resolution to the Armenian–Azeri conflict.

At the same time, the Council of Europe conferred the status of 'special guest' upon Azerbaijan in mid-1996. The Foreign Minister of Azerbaijan, Hasan Hasanov, declared that, after a transition period of three years, Azerbaijan would become the fortieth member state of this organization.[25] The failure of Azerbaijani laws to meet European standards and also mass violations of human rights are complicating Azerbaijan's entry into the Council of Europe. In January 1998, Azerbaijan's President Heydar Aliyev issued an instruction on the need to step up cooperation between Azerbaijan and the Council of Europe. The Azerbaijani Ministry of Foreign Affairs was instructed to ensure implementation of the program for cooperation between Azerbaijan and the Council of Europe and to allocate specialists to study all the Council of Europe documentation on human rights.[26] Azerbaijan, as a member of the Council, would receive permanent representation and become more effective in addressing disputes with Armenia.

While political matters have taken the forefront in Azerbaijan's relations with the European countries, economic issues remain important. The most prominent indicator of the development in economic relations is the rapid increase in European trade with Azerbaijan. Germany is Azerbaijan's most active European trading partner, followed by Italy and France.[27] (See Tables 6.4 and 6.5.) Increased trading patterns provide a bright outlook for the future of Azeri–European economic relations.

TABLE 6.4

AZERBAIJAN'S FOREIGN TRADE WITH CERTAIN EU MEMBER STATES ($,000)

Country	Exports	Imports
Germany	37,021	7,465
France	15,443	2,147
Italy	12,216	13,573
Finland	1,742	0
TOTAL	**66,422**	**23,185**

Source: EIU Country Reports, Georgia, Amenia, Azerbaijan (1st Quarter 1996).

TABLE 6.5

SHARES OF EUROPEAN COUNTRIES IN THE FOREIGN TRADE OF AZERBAIJAN IN 1994 ($,000)

Country	Total Foreign Trade	(%)
Germany	44,500	3.5
France	17,500	1.4
Italy	25,700	2.0
Finland	1,750	0.2
TOTAL	**89,450**	**7.1**

Source: Azerbaycan Ülke Raporu (Ankara: TIKA, 1995).

Kirgyzstan

Kirgyzstan's economic potential and rich resources base have not escaped the notice of European countries. Many European companies have invested in this Central Asian republic following its independence. The preferred means of gaining influence by European countries has been through economic and technical aid programs. For example, Switzerland included a promise of technical and economic aid in the framework of a cooperation agreement signed with Kirgyzstan in 1994. This agreement was signed by the President of Kirgyzstan, Askar Akayev, and his Swiss counterpart, Otto Stich, during Akayev's four-day official visit to Switzerland. According to this agreement, Switzerland would provide $5 million in financial aid for agriculture, forestry, privatization of public services and nongovernmental organizations.[28]

In the days following the signing of this cooperation agreement, a Swiss company set up a consortium with the Labor Council for the exploitation of precious-metal reserves in Retmen-Zoloto that will allow them to tap into the rich reserves in the city of Kara Balta. This consortium has since processed $2.3 million worth of raw metal, and expects to process 10 tons of gold, 16 tons of silver and other precious metals in this region.[29]

Kirgyzstan has also developed relations with Eastern European countries. A Kirghyz delegation headed by President Akayev traveled to Bulgaria in November 1994 for a meeting with the Bulgarian President Jelio Jelev. The two leaders signed economic and cultural cooperation agreements, and at the same time, the delegation initiated contacts with Bulgarian business leaders.[30]

Germany has also established good relations with Kirgyzstan. By June 1995 Germany had proposed approximately 250 commercial projects to Kirgyzstan valued at $1.5 million. The total cost of seven projects to be paid for by credits from the German government was $4.5 million.[31] As in Kazakhstan, Germany intends to look after an estimated 100,000 Kirghyz people of German descent by investing in Kirgyzstan. Among European nations, Germany is second in trading with Kirgyzstan, following the United Kingdom.[32] (See Table 6.6.)

Another consortium, which includes the European Bank for Reconstruction and Development, has extended a credit of $360 million to Kirgyzstan to develop gold mines in Kumtor.[33] These increased investments and interests in the former Soviet Republic are an indication of its increased economic importance to Europe.

TABLE 6.6

SHARES OF CERTAIN EU MEMBERS IN THE FOREIGN TRADE OF
KIRGYZSTAN IN 1994 (%)

Country	Exports	Imports
England	24.9	0.9
France	1.9	1.7
Germany	5.5	6.3
Italy	1.5	0.8
Holland	0.5	1.6
TOTAL	**34.3**	**11.3**

Source: EIU Country Profile, Kirygz Republic, 54 (1995–96).

Uzbekistan

The most active European investment to date in Uzbekistan has come from Germany and Italy. Some examples demonstrate the dynamic economic ties developing between this former Soviet Republic and the EU. For example, a joint venture was established between an Italian business (the Spinning-Silk Company) and the city of Margilan in Ferghan, which began production in August 1995.[34] The German government has donated medical and pharmaceutical products to the country worth DM20 million.[35] Uzbekistan's share of Germany's exportation credit for Russia and other countries of the CIS was

DM200 million in 1996.[36] France's Alcatel firm has also broken the Russian monopoly in telecommunication in Uzbekistan.

In 1993, Uzbekistan exported 415.5 million ECU in goods to EU countries. Imports from these countries totaled 201.5 million ECU. The importance of Uzbekistan's economic relationship with Europe is shown by the fact that 43.7 per cent of Uzbekistan's total exports and 47.7 per cent of its imports were with European countries.[37]

The European countries that enjoy the largest share of Uzbekistan's foreign trade are Germany, Italy and France, respectively. In 1995, Uzbekistan's trade with Italy doubled from that in 1994 and increased 2.5 times with Germany.[38] (See Table 6.7.) The noticeable increase in trade with Germany was the result of numerous economic endeavors, such as the building of roads that are suited to the needs of an independent state.[39]

Europe's interest in Uzbekistan was initially sparked by the country's gold. To reassure British investors about possible political instability that could jeopardize the exploration of gold, the Uzbek President Islam Karimov stated that they 'need not be afraid of anything happening in our country in the next five years because [I] will remain president'.[40]

Uzbekistan and Europe have also begun to strengthen their diplomatic ties. The joint committee of the Republic of Uzbekistan and the EU held its first meeting in Brussels in June 1995. The European Commission has announced that it will support Uzbekistan in its efforts to become a member of the World Trade Organization. The EU has also agreed to extend loan repayment schedules on finds used to purchase pharmaceutical products.[41]

TABLE 6.7
SHARES OF CERTAIN EU MEMBER STATES IN THE FOREIGN TRADE
OF UZBEKISTAN ($,000)

Country	Exports 1993	1994	Imports 1993	1994	Total 1993	1994
Germany	299,204	310,108	135,816	321,814	435,020	631,922
France	55,528	106,182	33,892	27,251	89,420	133,433
Italy	95,870	124,667	22,664	33,949	118,534	158,616
Finland	7,606	2,758	1,117	6,178	8,723	8,936
TOTAL	**458,208**	**543,715**	**193,489**	**389,192**	**651,697**	**932,907**

Source: EIU Country Reports, Kirygz Republic, Tajikistan, Turkmenistan, Uzbekistan 55 (1st Quarter 1996).

Turkmenistan

Britain was among the first European countries to establish economic relations with Turkmenistan. After a meeting between the Turkmen President Saparmurat Turkmenbasi and British investors on 28 February 1995, one member of the British delegation confirmed that they would undertake the exploitation of gold reserves.[42] Germany has also been active in Turkmenistan.

In June 1995, 17 important German corporations and finance organizations discussed cooperation in cereal processing, bread production, transport services and the textile industry with the relevant Turkmen ministries. This has led to ten joint ventures between German companies and Turkmen partners.[43] The TIKA (Turkish Development and Cooperation Agency) continues the study of the development of the 1,500-km Turkmen–Iran–Turkey gas pipeline project planned for the delivery of Turkmen gas to Europe over a 30-year period.

A significant part of Turkmenistan's $2.1 billion in exports and $1.5 billion in imports has been with European countries. According to available statistics, Germany and Italy dominate Turkmenistan's trade with Europe. (See Table 6.8.) In 1994, 19.2 per cent of Turkmenistan's foreign trade was with Germany, Italy, France and Finland. (See Table 6.9.)

TABLE 6.8

SHARES OF TURKMENISTAN'S TRADE WITH EUROPEAN COUNTRIES OUT OF ITS
TOTAL FOREIGN TRADE IN 1994 (%)

Country	Exports	Imports
Germany	1.6	4.1
Italy	1.7	3.8
Switzerland	2.1	
TOTAL	**5.4**	**7.9**

Source: Turkmenistan Ülke Raporu (1995).

TABLE 6.9

TURKMENISTAN'S FOREIGN TRADE WITH SOME MEMBER STATES OF
THE EU ($ '000)

Country	Exports		Imports		Total	
	1993	1994	1993	1994	1993	1994
Germany	37,079	40,116	45,593	89,268	82,672	129,384
France	43,147	49,109	2,725	6,903	45,872	56,012
Italy	63,355	98,969	60,233	54,649	123,588	153,618
Finland	28,816	6,333	1,286	6,491	30,102	12,824
TOTAL	**172,397**	**194,527**	**109,837**	**157,311**	**282,234**	**351,838**

Source: EIU Country Report (Kirgyz Republic, Tajikistan, Turkmenistan, Uzbekistan) 1st Quarter 1996.

OBSTACLES TO EXPANDED EUROPEAN RELATIONS WITH THE TURKIC REPUBLICS AND THE ROLE OF TURKEY

With this background of increased economic and political ties between Europe and the Turkic former Soviet republics, there is a growing need for the EU to re-evaluate its relations with Turkey. While the dramatic increase in economic ties strengthens the foundation for future relations, the increase in trade and commercial activity is not enough to ensure further progress, even with the political ties that have also developed. Relations with Turkey, as well as with Russia, will in many ways determine whether the promising economic opportunities between Europe and the Turkic republics will continue into the future.

First, European efforts to develop sustainable relations with the former Soviet republics have been conducted in the shadow of the potential threat of Russian intervention. Prior to 1993, Russia pursued a Western-oriented policy, but since then Russia has felt it necessary to revise its policy toward the West. This shift has primarily been motivated by efforts to expand NATO eastwards, as well as disappointment in the level of aid the West has provided. Russia is not ready to accept a Europe that comes close to its borders, and it perceives NATO expansion as a clear security threat.[44]

This situation includes the risk of coming face to face with Russia in any attempts by the EU to expand relations to the East. However, there is common agreement among the EU countries that concessions made to Russia given in return for its acceptance of NATO expansion will not include allowing it to act as it wishes in its 'near abroad'. This includes the promise not to exceed the limits established by the Treaty on Conventional Armed Forces in Europe, which seeks to reduce the level of ground troops in Europe. Ultimately, Europe's attitude toward any increase in Russian nationalist tendencies in its foreign policy will only be answered with time.

Turkey is also of great importance to the success of sustainable relations between Europe and the Turkic republics. Yet European governments have failed to recognize this fact. In the economic realm, both the European countries and the Turkic republics have expressed the desire to establish direct links, rather than indirect ones via Ankara.[45] Currently, only a limited amount of European capital and technology going to the Turkic republics does so through Turkey. The EU believes it can afford to overlook Turkey in its dealings with the Turkic republics. However, this may not be possible, particularly since the most important interest at stake – the proposed oil pipeline across Turkish territory to transport Azeri and Kazakh oil to Europe – has been stalled with little consensus to go forward.

This indifference toward the role Turkey can serve as an intermediary is a mistake. Some companies have been able to recognize the benefit Turkey's involvement in economic dealings with the Turkic republics can bring. For example, the president of the Greater Europa Group, an affiliate of Coca-Cola, said that, 'Turkey is a very powerful center' for entering the Turkic Republics, and that Coca-Cola has been 'very satisfied by the fact that [they] entered the market through Turkey', as it was 'a very wise decision'.[46] The entrepreneurial skills of Turkish nationals in Central Asia and Caucasia have come to the attention of many other multinational corporations, including

Caterpillar and Siemens. This has persuaded these companies to choose Istanbul as a way station in their efforts to develop economic ventures in these areas.

If Turkey's unsatisfactory progress with its application to join the EU is an indicator, it seems Europe does not want full cooperation with Turkey. Yet, as a 1997 article in the *New York Times* points out, 'Today, Europe's treatment of Turkey is a sensitive subject … in the broad band of Turkic nations that stretches across the Caucasus and Central Asia. The success or failure of Turkish efforts [to join the EU] is likely to affect perceptions of Europe across this region.'[47] In this regard, Turkey's integration with the EU would help diminish perceptions on the part of the Turkic republics that the EU may be prejudiced toward certain groups. It can be argued that attempts to block Turkey's membership into the EU can be attributed to Turkey's nature as an Islamic country, which only further provokes anti-Western attitudes.

On the other hand, the admission of Greece into the EU has had a harmful effect on potential relations with the Turkic republics. Greece persistently objects to any improvement in Turkish–EU relations. Close relations between Greece and Armenia increase distrust in the Turkic republics and may further add to regional tensions. The Greek perspective seems to ignore the fact that 'a European Turkey will be for Greece a much easier neighbor to live with than an alienated, fundamentalist and militaristic Turkey'.[48]

Islamic fundamentalism is perceived as a vital security issue in Europe. In this framework, Turkey can be of tremendous value in warding off the development of radical Islamic movements in the Turkic republics. While Iran and Pakistan are considered potentially dangerous influences, Turkey, because of its secular approach to government, can serve as a model state to these new republics.

The type of administration these former Soviet states prefer to emulate is the Western model. Secular values, democratic rights and the market economy are highly regarded in these countries. But, at the same time, the Islamist threat is recognized as real. During an official visit to the United Kingdom, the Prime Minister of Kirgyzstan stressed this by saying that, '[t]he spread of the extremist forms of Islam in Central Asia is a real danger, and the European Union should help us to prevent and reject this kind of extremism'.[49] Yet it is striking that it is not widely accepted in Europe that the EU should play an active role in staving off the spread of Islamic fundamentalism in these countries.

Beyond the entrepreneurial expertise of Turkish nationals with connec-tions to these republics and the ability of Turkey to serve as a secular model to the Turkic republics, remain the the undeniable cultural, linguistic, and reli-gious affinities between the Turkish people and the people of these new nations. Turkic-speaking people are in a sense a single people, ranging from Asia Minor far into Asia proper. The Turkish government recognizes this, and is aware of the benefits that can be derived from interaction with these 'sister nations'. Accordingly, Turkey has worked hard to develop relations with these countries. From the very beginning, Turkey has been aware that the keys to opening the gates of Asia are trade and education, and a cultural mobilization effort has been headed by nongovernmental organizations. Recent training and trade efforts by Turkey directed toward Central Asia demonstrate the emphasis on increasing the ties between these countries.

The integration of the Turkic republics with the modern world is also being pursued. For example, in roughly 200 high schools and 10 universities, English is used as the primary language of instruction.[50] These English-instruction schools developed from the initiative of Turkish civil societal organizations and are admired not only in Western circles, but also by Russian officials.[51]

Yet Turkey's efforts to expand relations with these republics have also had their shortcomings, particularly in providing economic aid, and in attempts to prevent Armenian aggression against Azerbaijan. In this sense Turkey is still too weak to play a 'big brother' role toward these republics, but the potential for the development of a wide-ranging meaningful relationshipship is great.

I suggest that Turkish politicians should consider the importance of Turkey in relations between Europe and the Turkic republics when pursuing their foreign-policy goals with Europe. Relations with the EU have been over-shadowed by the Kurdish question and human-rights problems, but should be re-evaluated and redefined in a more constructive way. The role of Turkey vis-à-vis the Turkic republics should be stressed in negotiations with the EU, and should be used to encourage the entry of Turkey into the EU. Former Prime Minister Tansu Çiller, responding to the Greek threat to veto Turkey's entry into the Customs Union, used this idea in her statement that '[Y]ou had better know that Turkey is coming with her population of 60 million and there are more than 200 million Turkic-speaking people behind her'.[52] Of course Turkey may not always succeed in mobilizing the Turkic republics behind it, but its importance to these republics and the benefits for Turkish foreign policy are undeniable.

The EU should strongly consider the consequences of denying Turkey's entrance into the Union. One commentator noted that, 'while the Central Asians recognize that Europe is of critical economic importance to them ... if Turkey itself is denied entry into the EU, how then could Turkey facilitate [Central Asia's] ties with Europe?'[53] In this respect, the deficiency in Turkey's economic institutions and resources could be compensated by giving priority to the long-term diplomatic reasoning that represents Turkey's integration to the EU.

CONCLUSION

The European countries seem to have succeeded in moving beyond Cold War parameters by adapting to developments following the dissolution of the Soviet Union. One of the clearest indicators of this transition is the rapid establishment of political and economic relations with the Turkic republics immediately following their independence. Overall, this has been done in a balanced manner, with a focus on the political, economic and military dimensions involved. In light of the discussions in this article, it is clear that at some times politics, and at other times economics, takes priority, yet of course they are interconnected.

Although Europe's economic relations with the Turkic republics have been relatively minor in terms of the EU's total trade, economic activity continues to expand. From the perspective of the Turkic republics, the importance of these relations is great. Relatively small figures in the total foreign trade of the EU could represent huge benefits for these new nations.

The success of continued sustainable economic and political relations between Europe and the Turkic republics also depends on the maintenance of positive relations with Turkey and active Turkish involvement in the process. This relationship can benefit Turkey itself as well. Its role as facilitator of relations between the two regions will enhance its bid to become integrated into the EU and will bring opportunities to share in the economic gains of cooperation. Furthermore, Turkey will benefit from the security that will be assured in the region from stability, cooperation and the maintenance of goodwill.

NOTES

1. See, for example, Pierre-Henri Laurent, 'European Integration and the End of the Cold War', in David Armstrong and Eric Goldstein (eds.), *The End of the Cold War* (1990), pp.147–8.
2. The Turkic republics are Kazakhstan, Azerbaijan, Krgyzstan, Uzbekistan and Turkmenistan.
3. See 'CSCE Accepts 10 New Members at the Prague Meeting', *Xinhua News Service*, 30 January 1992, available in LEXIS/NEXIS, Market Library, Promt File; Patrick Worsnip, 'Europe Welcomes 10 Ex-Soviet Republics to CSCE', *Reuters News Service*, 30 January 1992, available in LEXIS/NEXIS, Topnws Library, Reubsrn File; Daniel Snider, 'Ethnic Conflict in Ex-Soviet Region Keeps Riches out of Reach', *Christian Science Monitor*, 1 June 1995, p.7.
4. Gulnar Kendirbaeva, 'Time of Independence, Time of Trial', *Asian Affairs* 24, (1993), pp.280–1
5. European Commission, Europe in Figures (4th ed. 1995), p.398; see also European Commission, TACIS Contact Information (1994).
6. Most favored nation status was bestowed reciprocally. The agreement was submitted for approval to the EU Commission on 10 October 1994. See 'Prepared Testimony of Robert Gree Before the Senate Committee on Foreign Relations', *Federal News Service*, 13 June 1995, available in LEXIS/NEXIS, World Library, Allnws File.
7. See 'EC Report Weekly Diary', *Reuter EC Report*, 20 January 1995, available in LEXIS/NEXIS, World Library, Allwld File. See also *Cumhuriyet*, 25 January 1995; *Warsaw Voice*, 19 February 1995.
8. *New York Times*, 13 January 13, 1994, p.Dl; Ian McWilliam, '7 Major Oil Firms Sign Pact to Explore Caspian Energy', *Los Angeles Times*, 10 June 1993, p.Dl.

9. 'Eastern Promise', *Economist*, 25 Septmber 1993, p.47; Thomas Land, 'Energy-Rich Republics Set to Suck in Western Capital', *Gas World International*, May 1993, available in LEXIS/NEXLS, World Library, Allwld File.

10. Brian Killen, 'Kazakhstan, Western Oil Firms in Big Caspian Deal', Reuters Library Report, 3 December 1993, available in LEXIS/NEXIS, World Library, Allnws File.

11. Sander Thoenes, 'Kazakhstan Tries to Woo Disgruntled Gold Companies', *Financial Times*, 26 April 1996, 31 (mentioning the resulting cancellation by the government of Kazakhstan of the deal with the European Bank of Research and Development); *Turkish Daily News*, 11 January 1994.

12. See Thoenes, 'Kazakhstan Tries to Woo Disgruntled Gold Companies', p.31.

13. See Norman Peagam, 'Relying on Its Own Resources', *Euromoney*, (September 1994), pp.111–16.

14. Anatol Lieven, 'Russia After the Elections', *Washington Quarterly* (Winter 1997), p.39; *Country Profile: Comments and Analysis*, Quest Economics Database, January 1997, 3 (detailing the economic ties Kazakhstan has created with European countries).

15. Boris Sidorov, 'Near and Far in Russia 's Foreign Trade', *RusData DiaLine*, 5 January 1995, available in LEXIS/NEXIS, World Library, Allwld File.

16. Cihangir Boz, 'Turkiye Orta Asya Turk Cumhuriyetleri ve Almanya'nin Konumu' ('Turkey: Central Asian Turkic Republic Relations and Germany's Position') (1996) (unpublished MA thesis, Mannara University, Turkey). See also 'Germany Extends Another DM28.5m to Build More Housing for Ethnic Germans', *Info-Nova CIS Economics & Foreign Trade,* 13 September 1995, available in LEXIS/NEXIS, World Library, Allnws File; Steve Erlanger, 'Germany Pays to Keep Ethnic Germans in Russia', *New York Times*, 19 May 1993, Al. Evidence of this desire to emigrate existed prior to the break-up of the Soviet Union. 'Protest is Staged by Soviet Germans', *NewYork Times*, 17 November 1981, p.All.

17. *Country Profile: Comment & Analysis: Kazakhstan, Business Intelligence Report,* October 1996. See also 'Kazakhstan: Not out of the Woods Yet, Deutsche Bank Research', 27 September 1994, available in LEXIS/NEXIS, World Library, Allwld File.

18. *Turk Sanayici ve Isadamlari Beynelhalk Cemiyeti, Isadamlari Icin Azerbaycan El Rehberi 96* (1996) (The International Society of Turkish Industrialists and Businessmen, Azerbaijan Handbook for Businessmen 96)(hereinafter Azerbaijan Handbook), p.28

19. See Nikita Yermakov, 'Azeri President Signs Charter of Paris', *Russian Information Agency ITAR-TASS*, 21 December 1993, available in LEXIS/NEXIS, World Library, Allwld File.

20. See *Azerbaijan Handbook*, p.18.

21. 'Azerbaijan – Hope on the Horizon?', *Energy Economist*, January 1994, available in LEXIS/NEXIS, World Library, Allwld File.

22. 'Almanya'nin Azerbaycan Atagi' (Germany's Azerbaijan Attack), *Yeni Yuzyil*, 29 September 1995, p.11; 'Azerbaijan: Upgrading of the Power Generation Sector', *Industry Sector Analysis*, 9 May 1997, available in LEXIS/NEXIS, World Library, Allwld File.

23. 'German and Azerbaijani Foreign Ministers Discuss Cooperation', BBC Summary of World Broadcasts, 22 December 1995, available in LEXIS/NEXIS, World Library, Allwld File.

24. Ibid.

25. 'Azerbaijan Proposes Nagorno-Karabakh Autonomy', Reuters World Service, 6 June 1996, available in LEXIS/NEXIS, World Library, AlIwld File. See also 'Foreign Minister Hasanov Meets Council of Europe Officials', BBC Summary of World Broadcasts, 3 May 1997, available in LEXIS/NEXIS, World Library, Allwld File.

26. *Baku Turan*, in Russian, 1330 GMT, 22 January 1998 in *FBIS-SOV*-98-022, 27 January 1998.

27. 'Country Profile: Comment & Analysis: Azerbaijan', *Quest Economics Database*, April 1997, available in LEXIS/NEXIS, World Library, Allwld File.

28. See Konstantin Pribytkov, 'Swiss and Kyrgyz Presidents Sign Agreement on Technical Aid', Russian Information Agency 1TAR-TASS, 14 November 1994, available in LEXIS/NEXIS, World Library, Allwld File.

29. For a report concerning this operation, see Kartini Abd. Kadir and Zabrina Tahir, 'Malaysia: MOUs Establish Legal Framework for Trade Ties with Kyrgyz', *Business Times* (Malaysia), 21 July 1995, available in LEXIS/NEXIS, World Library, AliwId File.

30. 'Kyrgyz President's Visit: Treaties on Friendship and Economic Cooperation Signed', BBC Summary of World Broadcasts, 15 November 1994, available in LEXIS/NEXIS, World Library, AllwldFile.

31. See, generally, 'Forecast: Country Profile: Kyrghyzstan', *Quest Economics Database*, October 1996, available in LEXIS/NEXIS, World Library, Allwld File.

32. 'Commonwealth of Independent States, Around the Region', *Asian Review of Business & Technology*, 1 November 1995.

33. Anatoly Sukhonos, 'Foreign Currency from Subsoil', *RusData DiaLine*, April 1995, available in LEXIS/NEXIS, World Library, AlIwld File.

34. See 'Foreign Ministry Press Briefing', Official Kremlin International News Broadcast, 21 September 1995, available in LEXIS/NEXIS, World Library, AlIwld File.

35. For an overview of the program from the American perspective, see, generally, 'State Department Regular Briefing', *Federal News Service*, 4 November 1996, available in LEXIS/NEXIS, World Library, Allwld File.

36. 'Export Opportunities', *Journal of Commerce*, 29 January 1997, p.18C.

37. 'Country Profile: Comment & Analysis: Uzbekistan'.

38. Ibid.

39. See Fredrick Starr, 'Making Eurasia Stable', *Foreign Affairs* (January/February 1996), p.87.

40. Martha Brill Olcott, *Central Asia's New States: Independence, Foreign Policy and National Security* (1996), 135 Sergei Kliruschev, 'Testing the Mettle of Resourceful Central Asian Republics', *Asia Times*, 5 March 1997, available in LEXIS/NEXIS, World Library, Allwld File. See also Elif Kaban, 'Bankers Upbeat as Newmont Starts Uzbek Gold Project', Reuters Business Report, 25 May 1995, available in LEXIS/NEXIS, Topnws Library, Reubus File.

41. Michael S. Borish, 'Banking Reform in Transition Economies', *International Monetary Fund Finance and Development*, September 1995, p.23.

42. Richard M. Levine, 'Russia', *Mining Annual Review*, July 1995, p.169.

43. 'MEED Special Report: Oil & Gas', *Middle East Economist Digest*, 1 November 1996, p.27.

44. See, for example, 'National Press Club Morning Newsmaker Daniel Tarullo', *Fed. News Service*, 16 June 1997, available in LEXIS/NEXIS World Library, Allwld File.

45. Philip Robins, 'Between Sentiment and Self-Interest: Turkey's Policy Toward Azerbayan and the Central Asian States', *Middle East Journal 47*, (1993): 590; 'Turkey's Business World Wants Democracy', *Swiss Review of World Affairs*, 1 April 1997, available in LEXIS/NEXIS, World Library, AlInws File.

46. See Douglas Busvine, 'Coke Boosts Investments in Former Soviet Union', Reuters Business Report, 7 May 1996, available in LEXIS/NEXIS, Topnws Library, Reubus File.

47. Stephen Kinzer, 'Turkey Finds European Union Door Slow to Open', *New York Times*, 23 February 1997, p.A3.

48. Seyfi Tashan, 'A Turkish Perspective on Europe–Turkey Relations on the Eve of the IGC', *Foreign Policy* (Ankara), No. 20 (1996), pp.61–4.

49. Theodore Couloumbis and Prodrornos Yannas, 'Greek Security Challenges in the 1990s', in Gunay Goksu Ozdogan and Kernali Saybasili (eds.), *Balkans* (1995), p.212.

50. 'Turkish Motherland Party Leader Interviewed on Regional, Domestic Issues', BBC Summary of World Broadcasts, 12 December 1995, available in LEXIS/NEXIS, World Library, Allwld File.

51. Interview with Sergei Arutionov, Chairman of the Department of Caucasian Studies, Moscow Institute of Ethnology and Anthropology, Istanbul, Turkey, 4 October 1996.

52. Mustafa Aydin, 'Turkey and Central Asia: Challenges of Change', *Central Asian Survey*, (1996), p.165. For further information, see Ali Bora, 'Ekonomik Entegrasyon Surecinde Gumruk Birliginin Ekonomik Etkileri ve Avrupa Birligi' ('The Economic Effects of the Custom Union in the Economic Integration Process and the European Union') (1996) (unpublished MA thesis, Marmara University, Turkey).

53. Ibid.

CONCLUSION:
TURKEY'S OPTIONS

Numerous and significant changes have occurred in the world during the past ten years. The rise of the young democracies in Eastern Europe and the founding of independent states in Central Asia and Transcaucasia are among the visible and undoubtedly positive international results. These changes have also created conditions in which the need for cooperation and mutual understanding among countries is felt more acutely than ever.

A series of geopolitical relationships are emerging in Eurasia. On one side are Russia and Iran along with a series of smaller powers, including Greece and Armenia. On the other side are Turkey, Azerbaijan, Georgia, Ukraine and, as recent developments indicate, Israel. Also on the rise in the region is the influence and engagement of the United States and the European Union, both of which seek to tap into the vast energy reserves of the Caspian region. The emerging security environment is thus one in which two blocs of states are in increasing competition with one another. Therefore, policies that promote the further emergence of a bipolar order will have the potential to aggravate regional tensions and introduce new security concerns in this important yet unstable region.

In geopolitical environments in which competition rather than cooperation is the rule of the day, countries are quick to impute malevolent intentions upon their perceived adversaries, even if the adversaries' activities are ambiguous in nature. Moreover, under such conditions, all players are likely to view events in a zero-sum fashion in which a gain by one side is perceived as a loss by the other. Unfortunately, the Caucasus and Central Asia are emerging as such an environment.

In the current situation, in this first decade of the third millenium, it is still not possible to discuss a comprehensive Turkish foreign policy toward the Eurasian region. The main obstacle to adopting such a policy is the Turkish foreign-policy maker's lack of attention to the Caucasus and Central Asia as an international region and misperceptions about the environment in which this new international region is located. Instead, Turkey's Baku-based

2002

Caucasian and vague Central Asian policies have been built on an understanding of rivalry vis-à-vis Iran and Russia.

In addition, Turkish foreign policy has become hostage to the Kurdish
problem and its Azerbaijani policy. It is possible to classify Ankara's policy
toward the region as a security-first policy with a myopic vision of Iran and
Russia as the main enemies of Turkey, among others, providing a motivation
for this overriding emphasis on security.

Russia, Iran and to a smaller extent Ukraine and Uzbekistan are the most
important countries to be taken into consideration in the formulation of a new
policy toward the Eurasian region. Turkish–Russian relations are especially
significant in terms of demonstrating the dynamism of business people and the
relative impotency of governmental bureaucracies in their inability to catch up
with the pace of their people. Official Ankara and Moscow not only lag far
behind the developments of people-to-people relations, but they have further
hampered economic development by their slow pace in the preparation of
requisite legal foundations. While government officials have been hampered
by their tendency to continue to formulate official policies in accordance with
anachronistic ideas of regional power rivalries and conflicting interests,
unofficial shuttle trade has risen almost to the level of official trade and
mutually profitable business opportunities have been seized by innovative
business people on both sides. This argument is also valid in terms showing
Turkish society's dynamism in the Caucasus and Central Asia.

With respect to the Ukraine and Uzbekistan, prospects for the future are
brighter than is the case with either Iran or Russia. Despite current severe
economic and political crises, Ukraine and Uzbekistan are likely to emerge as
influential countries that will have a powerful voice in the future political and
economic shape of the Black Sea region and of the Central Asia. The Ukraine
is a good candidate for a strong ally of Turkey. Its very existence as an independent nation and its pro-Western orientation provide relief to Turkish
policy makers, though they are not sure how to utilize the relation in terms of
regional politics.

A close look at Turkey's policy toward Russia and Iran makes it obvious
that Turkish policy has also to a considerable extent become hostage to its
policy toward Azerbaijan in the regional context. The so-called conflicting
interests between Turkey and these two states mainly emerge from Turkey's
loyalty to the Azeri side in all controversies, especially the legal-status debate
over Caspian pipeline politics and the Karabakh question. If one questions
what Turkey has gained from this stance, it is difficult to see that it has gained
anything other than increasing its prospects for a possible Baku–Ceyhan
project. The first premise of a new Turkish foreign policy should be to gain a
tactical friendship with at least one of these two countries. Turkey cannot
successfully pursue a regional rivalry, taking internal and external restrictions
into consideration, against both Iran and Russia, even if we forget the fact that

there is more reason for cooperation than for conflict. With respect to the prospect of antagonizing Russia, one may also question the rationality of jeopardizing the current volume of trade and business opportunities that Turkey enjoys with Russia for the mere possibility of a project that would probably yield profit only in coming decades. This does not mean that Ankara should give up its attempts to have a share of the Caspian riches, but it should be able to pursue multifaceted policies. Turkish foreign policy makers should go steady on the implementation of this project and should not propose any other option. It should be noted that, even after the AIOC's probable decision to choose Baku–Ceyhan as the major pipeline route (or one of them), such a decision will not mean that Azeri oil will flow through Turkish territory. There will still be many more obstacles for Ankara to cross before realizing its ambitions in the Caspian region. In case of AIOC's refusal of Baku–Ceyhan option, it should be kept in mind that this project will continue to have potential for the rest of Caspian oil.

The second cornerstone of Turkish policy should be to develop a more rational and sensitive approach toward ethnic entities in the region. Suffering from terrorist insurgency in its heartland, the Turkish approach to cases of ethnic unrest in the region should be to support the sovereignty and integrity of states and to offer mediation in the case of severe crises. This policy of increased sensitivity should be applied to Crimean Tatars, Chechens, Abkhazians, Acaras and other less populous ethnic identities keeping the fact in mind that coming years will witness increasing micronationalist movements all over the world. The third leg of a new policy should be to initiate and encourage intra-regional economic and political projects. The Ukranian pipeline project through Anatolia, Russian and Iranian gas pipeline projects and the Turkmen gas project are of considerable importance for Turkey. In particular, these represent the sole feasible options that Ankara has to provide gas to the central and eastern parts of Turkey. These projects are viable and involve no third-party dimension that might create unexpected difficulties.

The fourth component of this strategy would be to reconsider the Turkish position toward US policy in the region and to reformulate the Turkish position vis-à-vis this policy in the light of Turkish state interests. In fact, an aggressive US policy may be a source of instability and further polarization in the region. The current US approach to see Turkey, the Ukraine, Georgia and Azerbaijan as its regional allies and its policies towards the Caspian Sea region promise may be self-destructive to its own interests. The US policy that seeks to exploit friction between Russia and Turkey, and Turkey and Iran, in order to limit the roles of Moscow and Tehran in regional politics may also be a source of tension and instability for the entire region.

A fifth component would be an attempt to cool down security concerns throughout the region. Russia amassed troops on its Caucasian borders in excess of the limits established by the 1990 Conventional Forces in Europe treaty (CFE), asserting that Russia's current security needs required an even greater presence in the region than was necessary during the Soviet period.[1] Russia had previously expressed the desire to increase its forces in the area to 2,000 tanks, 5,000 armored vehicles and 2,500 artillery pieces, an amount well over the limit set by the CFE.[2] In addition, the issue of NATO's expansion toward the East is another source of concern, since the Russian political elite have no desire to share a border with their former enemy's troops. In the post-Soviet era, good relations with the Russian Federation have gained more importance for Turkey than had been the case in the Cold War period. On the one hand, it is contrary to Turkey's interests to have a new line of division in Europe. But on the other hand, if the West gives Russia a free hand with respect to the former USSR republics (which Russians call the 'near abroad'), that is also a matter for Turkey's concern. Turkey should use its partnership in NATO wisely to make sure that Russia does not exceed agreed-upon limits of military presence in the Caucasus and also that NATO's expansion does not antagonize Russia, strengthening the hands of brown-red factions in Moscow.

A sixth facet of this new policy should focus upon the ever-present need to settle the region's many political disputes, the bloodiest of which have been the Armenian–Azerbaijani war and the Chechen conflict. In terms of the latter, Ankara and Moscow need to reach an understanding not to intervene in each other's 'internal problems' and not to turn the situation into a zero-sum game. As for the Karabakh conflict, relations with Armenia may seem less important for Turkey in comparison with other nations, but peace itself in the Caucasus has an enormous value, not only for Turkey but for all interested parties as well. While Armenia's policy toward Turkey has been hostage to history, Turkish policy has been hobbled by its concern for the Azerbaijani position in the conflict. The current deadlock in the peace process speaks to the necessity for a more active Turkish role, with greater independence from the Azeri position in the conflict. Ankara needs more room to maneuver in its relations with Armenia; this seems to be the only way to bring Armenia to the bargaining table. In this delicate environment, a more balanced posture on the part of Turkey might encourage Baku toward the kind of greater compromise that appears to be necessary for a peaceful solution. A more even-handed Turkish approach would also strengthen the hands of liberals in Armenia and encourage them to change their stance with respect to peace negotiations. As a US Deputy Secretary of State emphasized in October 1998: 'It is now time for Turkey and Armenia to consider what further steps might be taken to build a stronger, more stable bilateral relationship.'[3]

Finally, Turkish policy should utilize the Black Sea Economic Cooperation Zone project as an international forum for addressing the problems of the region from a broader geopolitical perspective and to mobilize support for relevant domestic actors. In its current form, political leaders and foreign-policy makers are the principal decision makers in the project. If one looks at the national security politics of member states, it can be observed that, in most cases, these policies do not reflect the intrinsic national interests of the populations of member states. State policies are not dictated by rational choices, which would demand an end to these conflicts, and lack the required elasticity to adapt to ever-changing environments. The Black Sea region is in the process of 'becoming' a subregion and formulating a distinctly new identity. With its current structure, the state-dominated approach to the project promises nothing more than a loose political organization with little prospect of evolving into a genuine economic union.

The key for Russia, Azerbaijan, Turkey and each of the other states with a stake in the outcome of these controversies is to view one another as a partner rather than a rival and to realize that, when another country among them benefits from an economic opportunity and furthers its prosperity, this does not represent a loss to the others. Rather, the domestic stability that prosperity on the part of one country facilitates will ensure every other country in the region the opportunity to develop and prosper in its own right, free from the threat of opportunistic aggression. What is more, Turkey is on the threshold of a transformation that will open new horizons in both domestic and foreign politics. More and more emphasis will be placed on encouraging links with the Balkans, the Middle East and the ex-Soviet, Turkic republics, rather than insisting on the idea of a 'Fortress Turkey'. The current mentality – based on the early-twentieth-century European model of the nation state – does not seem relevant to the coming century. In order to secure a viable place for itself in the twenty-first century, Turkey's establishment will have to cultivate the ability to recognize necessary change and take a great leap forward in respecting the dynamism of its own society. Otherwise, Turkish foreign policy will continue to be held hostage to domestic political considerations and will have little chance to play a constructive role in the future of regional or international politics.

NOTES

1. Odile Meuvret, 'Russia Scuppers Conventional Arms Limition Talks', Agence France Presse, 16 Novevmber 1995.
2. Brooks Tigner, 'Force Levels Hike Turk, Russian Friction', *Defense News*, 26 November 1995, p.4.
3. Strobe Talbott, 'U.S.–Turkish Relations in an Age of Interdependence', speech to the Washington Institute For Near East Policy, Willard Inter-Continental Hotel, Wednesday, 14 October 1998.

SELECT BIBLIOGRAPHY

Abromowitz, M., 'Turkey After Ozal', *Foreign Policy*, No. 91 (Summer 1993), pp.164–81

Adams, T. and Rich, G., 'Great Power Politics and the Azerbaijan Oil Pipeline', *Washington Institute of Near East Policy: Policy Watch*, 24 February 1997, http://www.washingtoninstitute.org/watch/Policywatch/policywatch1997/237.htm.

Altstadt, A., *The Azerbaijani Turks: Power and Identity Under Russian Role*, Stanford: Hoover Institution, 1992.

Apostolou, A., 'New Players in an Old Game', *The Middle East*, No. 213 (July 1992), p.25.

Aras, B., 'Azerbaijan's Far Eastern Friends', *Middle East International 570*, 13 March 1998, p.16

Azerbaijan, Baku: UNDP Azerbaijan, 1996.

Azerbaijan: An Economic Profile. Springfield, V.A.: Library of Congress Documents Expediting Project, 1995.

Blank, S.J., 'Turkey's Strategic Engagement in the Former USSR and US Interests', in Stephen J. Blank, Stephen C. Pelletiere and William T. Johnsen (eds), *Turkey: Strategic Position at the Crossroads of World Affairs*, Carlisle Barracks, PA: Strategic Studies Institute, 1993.

Bolukbasi, S., 'The Controversy Over the Caspian Sea Mineral Resources: Conflicting Perceptions, Clashing Interests', *Europe–Asia Studies* 50, No. 3 (May 1998), pp.397–414.

Croissant, M. P., 'Turkey and NATO After the Cold War', *Strategic Review* 23, No. 4 (Fall 1995).

Din, H. and Mian, A., 'An Analysis of the Foreign Economic Policies of the Central Asian States and Azerbaijan: 1992–1996', Fletcher School of Law and Diplomacy: Unpublished PhD Thesis, 1997.

Economist Intelligence Unit Country Report: Azerbaijan, London: *The Economist*, 1998.

Federov, Y., 'Russia's Policies Toward Caspian Region Oil: Neo Imperial or

Pragmatic II?' *Perspectives on Central Asia* (October 1996), http: //www.cpss.org/casianw/octpers.html.

Forstythe, R., *The Politics of Oil in the Caucasus and Central Asia*, Adelphi Papers, No. 40. Oxford: International Institute for Strategic Studies, 1996.

Fuller, G. E., 'Turkey's New Eastern Orientation', in Graham E. Fuller and Ian O. Lesser (eds), *Turkey's New Geopolitics: From the Balkans to Western China*, Boulder: Westview Press, 1993, pp.37–98.

Fuller, G. E. and Lesser, I.O. (eds), *Turkey's New Geopolitics: From the Balkans to Western China*, Boulder: Westview Press, 1993.

Goldstein, L., 'Conflict in the Caucasus may Escalate', *Harvard International Review* 16, No. 1 (Fall 1993), pp.42–6.

Gultekin, N. B. and Mumcu, A., 'Black Sea Economic Cooperation', in Vojtech Mastny and R. Craig Nation (eds), *Turkey Between East and West*, Boulder: Westview, 1996.

Hale, W., 'Turkey, the Black Sea and Transcaucasia', in John F. R. Wright, Suzanne Goldenberg and Richard Schofield (eds), *Transcaucasian Boundaries*, New York: St Martin's, 1996.

Hunter, S. T., 'The Muslim Republics of the Former Soviet Union: Policy Challenges for the United States', *The Washington Quarterly* 15, No. 3 (Summer 1992), pp.57–71.

Iskit, T., 'Turkey: A New Actor in the Field of Energy Politics', *Perceptions* 1, No. 1 (March–May 1996).

Kasenov, O., 'Russia, Transcaucasia, and Central Asia: Oil, Pipelines, and Geopolitics', in Roald Z. Sagdeev and Susan Eisenhower (eds), *Central Asia: Conflict, Resolution, and Change*, Chevy Chase: CPSS Press, 1997.

Khan, M., 'External Threats and the Promotion of a Trans-National Islamic Consciousness: The Case of the Late Ottoman Empire and Contemporary Turkey', *Islamic World Report* 1, No. 1 (1996).

Kirisci, K., 'New Patterns of Turkish Foreign Policy Behavior', in Cigdem Balim, *et al.* (eds), *Turkey: Political, Social and Economic Challanges in the 1990s*, Leiden: E.J.Brill, 1995.

Landau, J. M., *Pan-Turkism: From Irredentism to Cooperation*, Bloomington: Indiana University Press, 1995.

Lesser, I. O., 'Bridge or Barrier? Turkey and the West After the Cold War', in Graham E. Fuller and Ian O. Lesser (eds), *Turkey's New Geopolitics: From the Balkans to Western China*, Boulder: Westview Press, 1993, pp.99–140.

Lipovsky, I. P., 'Central Asia: In Search of a New Political Identity', *Middle East Journal* 50, No. 2 (Spring 1996), pp.211–23.

Mackenzie, K., 'Azerbaijan and the Neighbors', *World Today* 48, No. 1 (January 1992).

Mufti, M., 'Daring and Caution in Turkish Foreign Policy', *Middle East Journal* 52, No. 1 (Winter 1998), pp.32–50.

Onis, Z., 'The Political Economy of Islamic Resurgence in Turkey: The Rise of Welfare party in Perspective', *Third World Quarterly* 18, No. 4 (Fall 1997), pp.743–67.

Ozdag, U., 'Kuzey Irak ve PKK' (Northern Iraq and PKK) *Avrasya Dosyasi* 3, No. 1 (Spring).

Ozuye, O., 'Black Sea Economic Cooperation', *Mediterranean Quarterly* 3, No. 3 (Summer 1992), pp.48–54.

Peimani, H., *Regional Security and the Future of Central Asia: The Competition of Iran, Turkey and Russia*, Westport: Greenwood Publishing, 1998.

Pompfret, R., 'The Economic Cooperation Organization: Current Status and Future Prospects', *Europe–Asia Studies* 49, No. 4 (June 1997), pp.657–68.

Robins, P., 'Between Sentiment and Self-Interest: Turkey's Policy Toward Azerbaijan and the Central Asian States', *Middle East Journal* 47, No. 4 (Autumn 1993), pp.593–610.

Rumer, B. Z., 'The Gathering Storm in Central Asia', *Orbis* 37, No. 1 (Winter 1993), pp.89–105.

Shoumikhin, A., 'Economics and Politics of Developing Caspian Oil Resources', *Perspectives on Central Asia* (November 1996), http://www.cpss.org/casianw/novpers.html.

Shoumikhin, A., 'New Developments Related to Caspian Oil', *Perspectives on Central Asia*, (December 1996), http://www.cpss.org/casianw/canews.htm.

Statistical Handbook 1994: States of the Former USSR, Studies of Economies in Transformation, Paper No. 14, Washington, DC: The World Bank, 1994

Talbott, S., 'U.S.–Turkish Relations in an Age of Interdependence', Speech to the Washington Institute For Near East Policy, Willard Inter-Continental Hotel Wednesday, 14 October 1998

Tirman, J., 'Improving Turkey's Bad Neighborhood', *World Policy Journal* 15, No. 1 (Spring 1998), pp.60–8.

Winrow, G. M., 'Turkey's Role in Asian Pipeline Politics', *Jane's Intelligence Review* 9, No. 2 (February 1997).

INDEX

110